We acknowledge the Traditional Owners of this Country. We pay our respects to Kaurna Elders past and present, and recognise their deep and ongoing connection to this place. We desire to walk together into a better future—one with healing, reconciliation and environmental restoration at its core.

SEP 2024 APR 2025

CHIHULY

IN THE

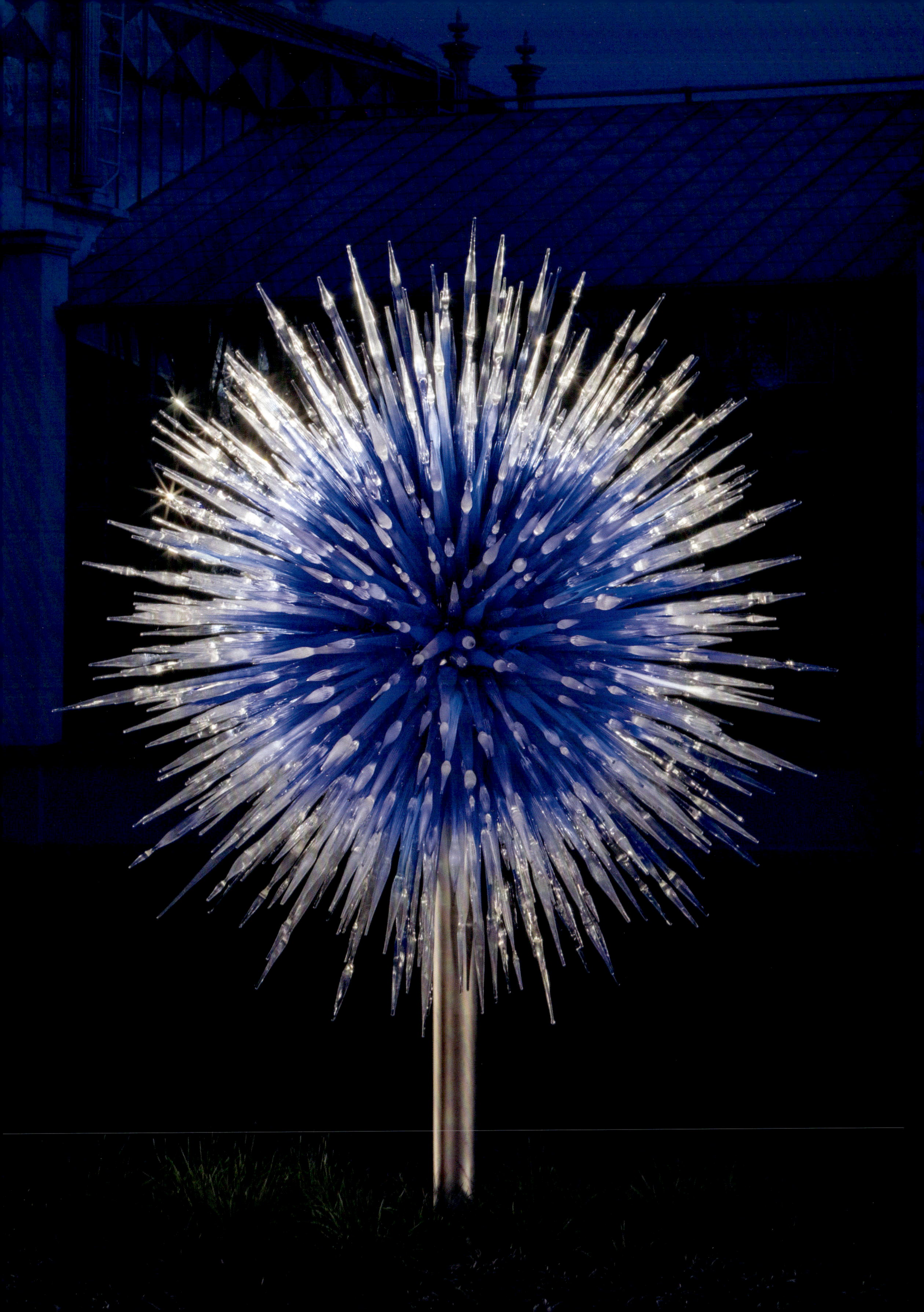

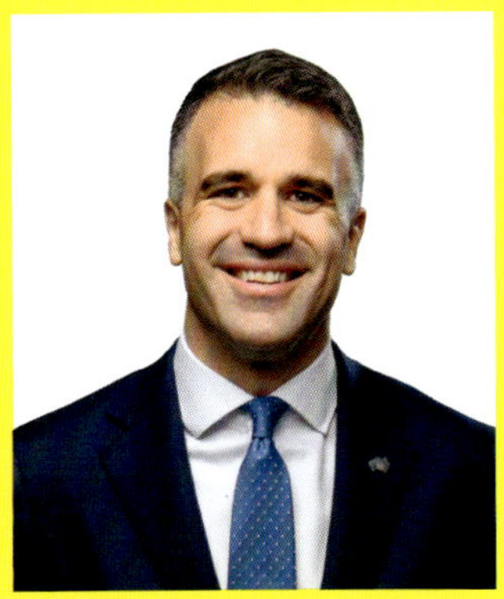

A message from the Premier of South Australia

South Australia has a long and celebrated history of delivering world-leading major events, and I'm delighted to welcome *Chihuly in the Botanic Garden* to the ever-growing list.

Over the summer of 2024/25, our beautiful Adelaide Botanic Garden hosts this truly remarkable, Australian-first exhibition of incredible sculptures by the world's master of contemporary glass.

We are delighted that Dale Chihuly has chosen our city for his first major botanic garden exhibition in Australia, seeing us join gardens in the USA, London and Singapore to host one of these projects at spectacular scale.

Adelaide truly is the perfect choice for what will be a drawcard for thousands of visitors from near and far, as this exhibition adds to our stacked events calendar, providing yet another excellent reason to visit South Australia.

From the VAILO Adelaide 500 to the AFL Gather Round, through to the Adelaide Festival, Adelaide Fringe and WOMADelaide, we have no shortage of attractions, and everyone attending these events will have the extreme good fortune to come and see what will be a truly memorable and striking outdoor exhibition.

If you are travelling to Adelaide, I hope you enjoy your stay, and also get the chance to explore our state and experience the best South Australia has to offer, from stunning natural beauty, world-renowned wine regions and a flourishing food and wine industry, to regional centres brimming with activities and attractions.

For South Australians, this is a chance to see our Botanic Garden through a new lens. We can also take pride in the focus that *Chihuly in the Botanic Garden* will bring to our local glass art community, reflecting that we have here a true centre of excellence in the art form and perfectly showcased by project partner JamFactory.

I know that a huge amount of work, in both Seattle and Adelaide, has gone into this project and I congratulate all who have been involved in planning, staging and supporting this spectacular exhibition.

Hon. Peter Malinauskas MP
Premier of South Australia

Jet and Crimson Fiori (detail), 2024
178 x 168 x 135 cm

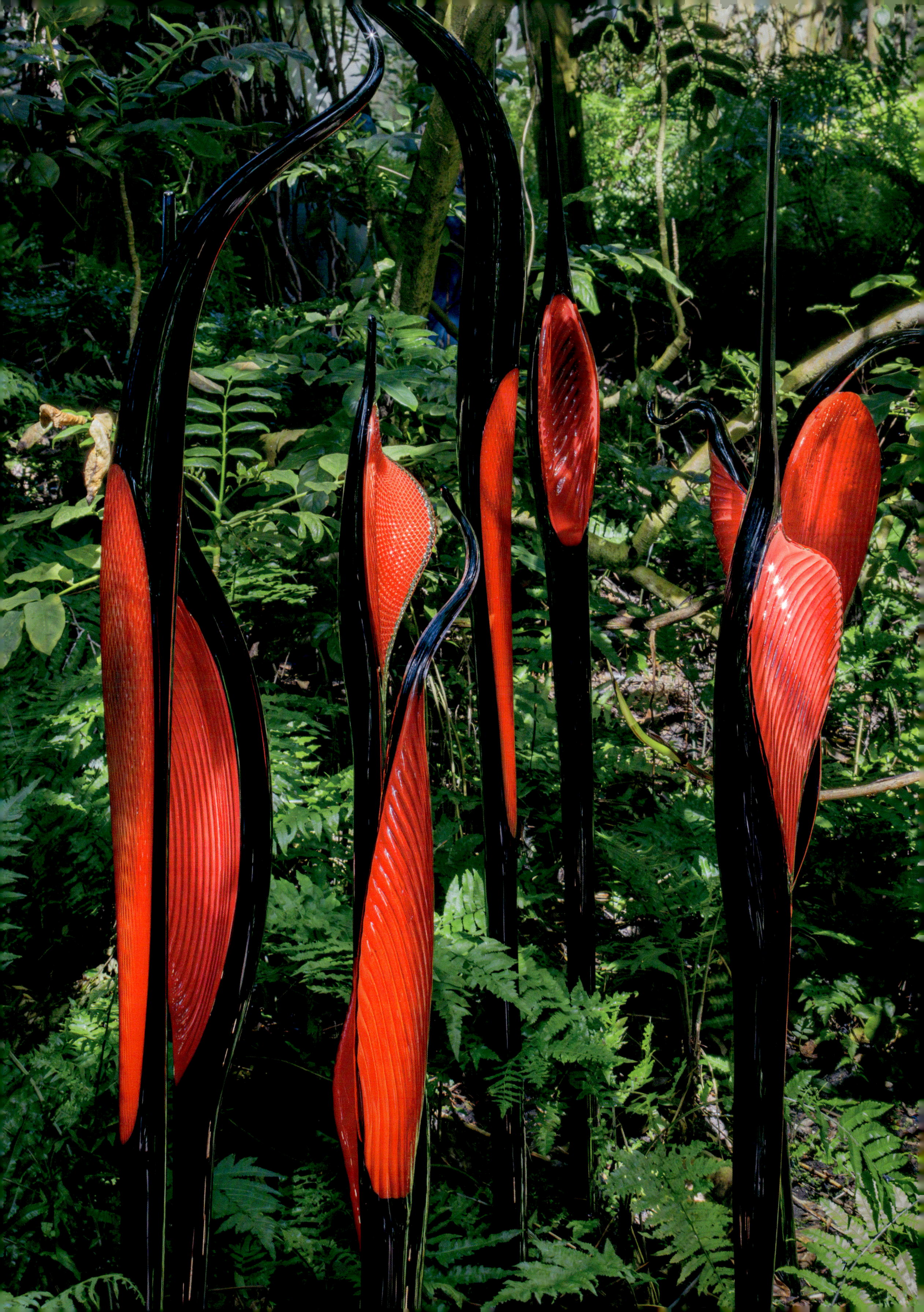

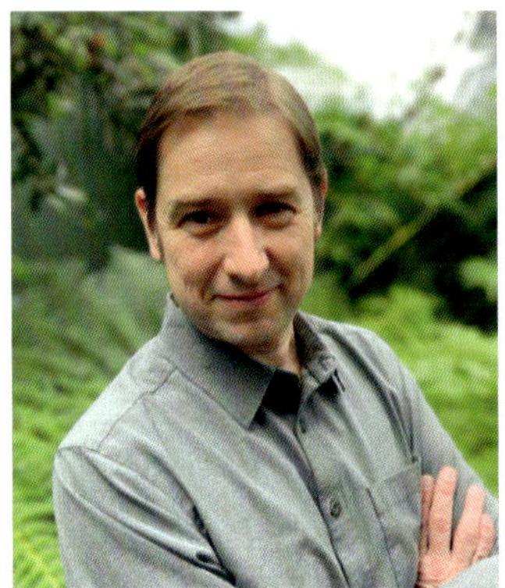

Photo: Alison Frappell

A reflection: Dale Chihuly and Botanic Gardens

I can still remember my first encounter with a Dale Chihuly artwork. I was working in London and visited the Victoria and Albert Museum (V&A), which had recently carried out renovations on its main entry foyer. Soaring above the central information desk was this astonishing concoction of blue and yellow twisted glass. It looked at once alive, anarchic and completely at odds with the formal building which housed it. Somehow it also looked exactly 'right' there—11 metres of blown glass hanging from the building's ceiling dome, playing with both light and shadow and creating a completely new sense of space.

A couple of years later Chihuly, who had been working with a series of botanical gardens in the USA, brought his first international *Garden Cycle* collection to London's iconic Kew Gardens. This time the works were displayed in outdoor spaces, among the living plant collections—and this time I could see the full diversity of what Chihuly and his studio team could do with blown glass. There were floating works—inspired by Japanese fishing floats, but in every kind of colour—and a boat filled with a riot of glass reeds and flowers reflected in the water. There were gold and green chandeliers in the glasshouses; I was later to learn that Dale Chihuly's fascination with botanic gardens stemmed in part from the glass conservatories used to grow and display botanical collections.

And there were people—so many people. The sense of joy and delight the visitors had in the interaction between these works and the gardens' spaces, collections and architecture was palpable. *Gardens of Glass: Chihuly at Kew* was one of the highlights of 2005 in London's cultural calendar—filling the gardens with curious visitors and providing a genuine challenge to London's galleries, museums and mega-musicals for the tourists' attention.

It is the relationship between art, nature, tradition and gardens that has driven Dale Chihuly's series of botanic garden projects, a series that spans over twenty years and reaches across the globe. Starting with the Garfield Park Conservatory in Chicago in 2001, this exhibition cycle has populated gardens and glasshouses at over 20 different botanic garden sites, each with their own unique character and context to be explored with the glass forms that Dale and his team create.

The opportunity that we have in Adelaide to bring Dale Chihuly's collection here, on beautiful Kaurna Country, with support from the South Australian Government, is a special one for all of us. Adelaide is only the third city outside the USA, after London's Kew Gardens and Singapore's Gardens by the Bay, to do so and the logistics and preparation that goes into such an undertaking are substantial indeed. The work that both the Chihuly Studio and our team here at the Adelaide Botanic Garden have put into this project has been extraordinary. We have seen first-hand the care that Dale and his team take in situating the works in the landscape and the consideration of both the living collection and the architecture in

Cobalt Frog Feet (detail), 2024
175 x 272 x 196 cm

which the pieces are nestled. Our own team have responded to the challenge of hosting the collection with new plantings to complement the works, and an extensive public and education program to bring together these twin threads of art and nature.

One of the things I love about botanic gardens the world over is their variety—both in the rich diversity of their collections and in their varied moods and spaces. Historically, horticulturalists, botanists and designers have created gardens and herbaria that tell stories, invite contemplation and drive the gathering of new knowledge and understanding. Their evolution from formal 'exclusive' spaces to open scientific institutions connected with their communities is an ongoing one.

In the Adelaide Botanic Garden's 50 hectares, you can lose yourself in the Australian Forest and forget you are a 15-minute walk from Rundle Mall. Adelaide's distinct seasons give the garden a rich variety of experiences—the sudden bloom of the Wisteria Arbours, the slow unfurling of the lotus in the Nelumbo Pond and the emergence of all the garden birds with their different seasonal rhythms. Dale Chihuly's work invites us to see the Garden in yet another light and creates an extraordinary experience which will live on in visitors' memories, just like my 20-year recollection of the ceiling of the V&A.

To the extraordinary people at Chihuly Studio, to our supporters here in Adelaide and to our talented and dedicated staff and volunteers, thank you all!

Michael Harvey

Director, Botanic Gardens and State Herbarium

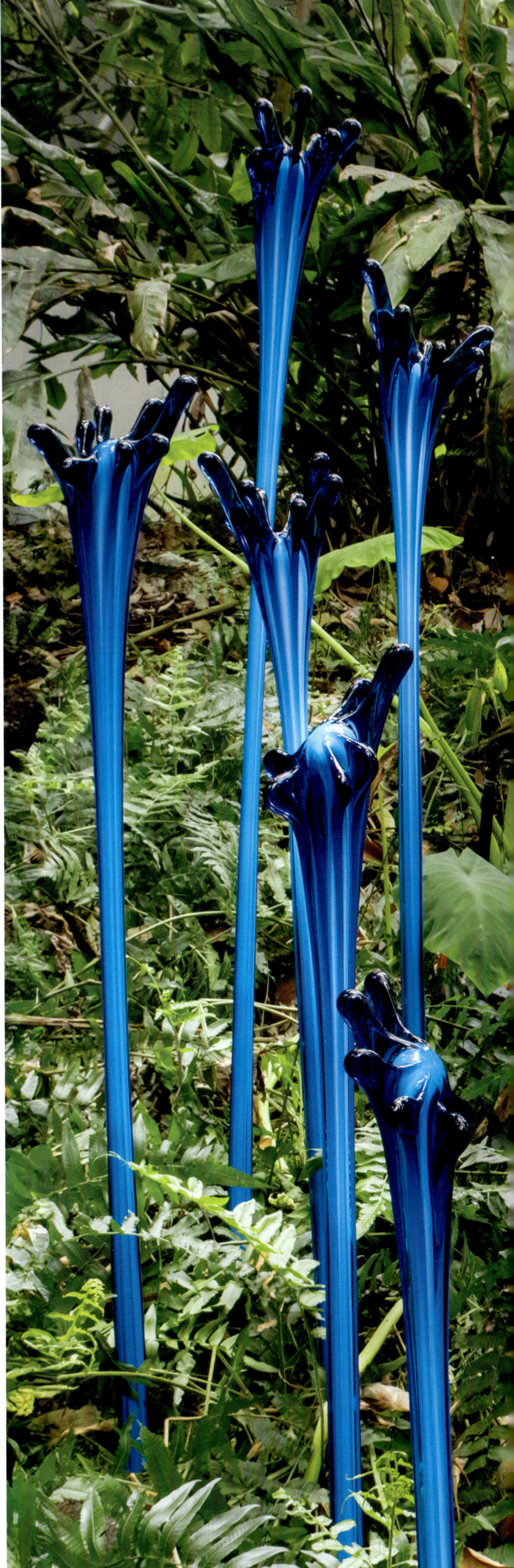

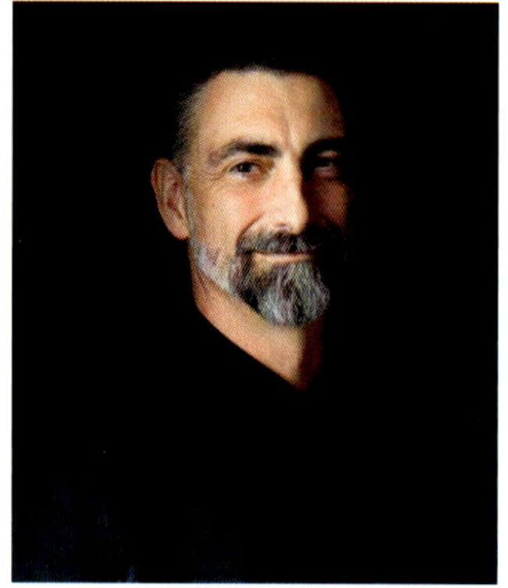

Photo: Connor Patterson

Adelaide and Seattle—cities of glass

It is fitting that this latest iteration of Dale Chihuly's *Garden Cycle* is taking place exclusively in Adelaide. Not only is our Botanic Garden a remarkable backdrop for Chihuly's spectacular glass installations, but the city of Adelaide itself is considered a major centre for glass art globally. The epic scale of *Chihuly in the Botanic Garden* and its promotion as a major event over seven months on the national cultural calendar will draw significant attention to glass as a material for creative expression and shine a spotlight on the thriving glass art ecosystem that exists in South Australia.

Coinciding with *Chihuly in the Botanic Garden*, 2024 marks 50 years of glass at JamFactory—Adelaide's nation-leading not-for-profit craft and design centre. In 1974, just a year after the organisation was founded by the Don Dunstan-led State Government, the JamFactory Glass Studio was set up by its first Studio Head. Like Chihuly, Sam Herman had been a student of Harvey Littleton—widely considered the earliest pioneer of the modern studio glass movement.

Today, JamFactory's Glass Studio is the busiest open-access glassblowing studio in the Southern Hemisphere. Two large furnaces, each with 450kg capacity, provide an almost constant supply of molten glass for the 40 or so artists who regularly hire the facility to make their own work and for the many glassblowers JamFactory employs to produce glassware, lighting, awards, trophies and other bespoke glass pieces for a wide variety of clients. Importantly, the Studio also offers a deeply immersive two-year training program, which provides unparalleled access to glassblowing time and attracts emerging artists from around the world. Visitors to JamFactory can watch glassblowing live every day from a dedicated viewing platform.

Undoubtedly the best-known glassblower in Adelaide is Nick Mount. Few, if any, individuals have had more influence on glass art and design in Australia over the past 50 years. In 1974 Mount met American glass artist Richard Marquis, who had been brought to Australia by the Australia Council to demonstrate glassblowing and advise on the establishment of glass courses. Marquis was one of two Americans to travel to Venini Fabrica in Venice in the late 1960s (Dale Chihuly in 1968 and Marquis the following year) to learn the then-closely guarded Venetian glassblowing techniques. Newly wed, Mount and his wife Pauline were engaged as assistants to Marquis and accompanied him on a seminal demonstration tour of Victoria and Tasmania. When Mount was appointed as Head of JamFactory's Glass Studio in 1994, he introduced training and production methodologies and a particular work ethic that continue to strongly influence JamFactory's operations today.

South Australia remains one of only three locations in Australia where glass can be studied formally at a tertiary level. The first glass program was initiated by artist Stephen Skillitzi (who had taken a class taught by Dale Chihuly at the Haystack Mountain School of Crafts in 1968) not long after he began teaching ceramics at the South Australian School of Art in 1976. Gerry King and Abraham Fynnaart set up a separate program at the South Australian College of Advanced Education in the early 1980s, with both programs ultimately absorbed into one within what is now known as the University of South Australia. This enduring glass program has launched the careers of many prominent artists, including Yhonnie Scarce, Liam Fleming and current JamFactory Glass Studio Head

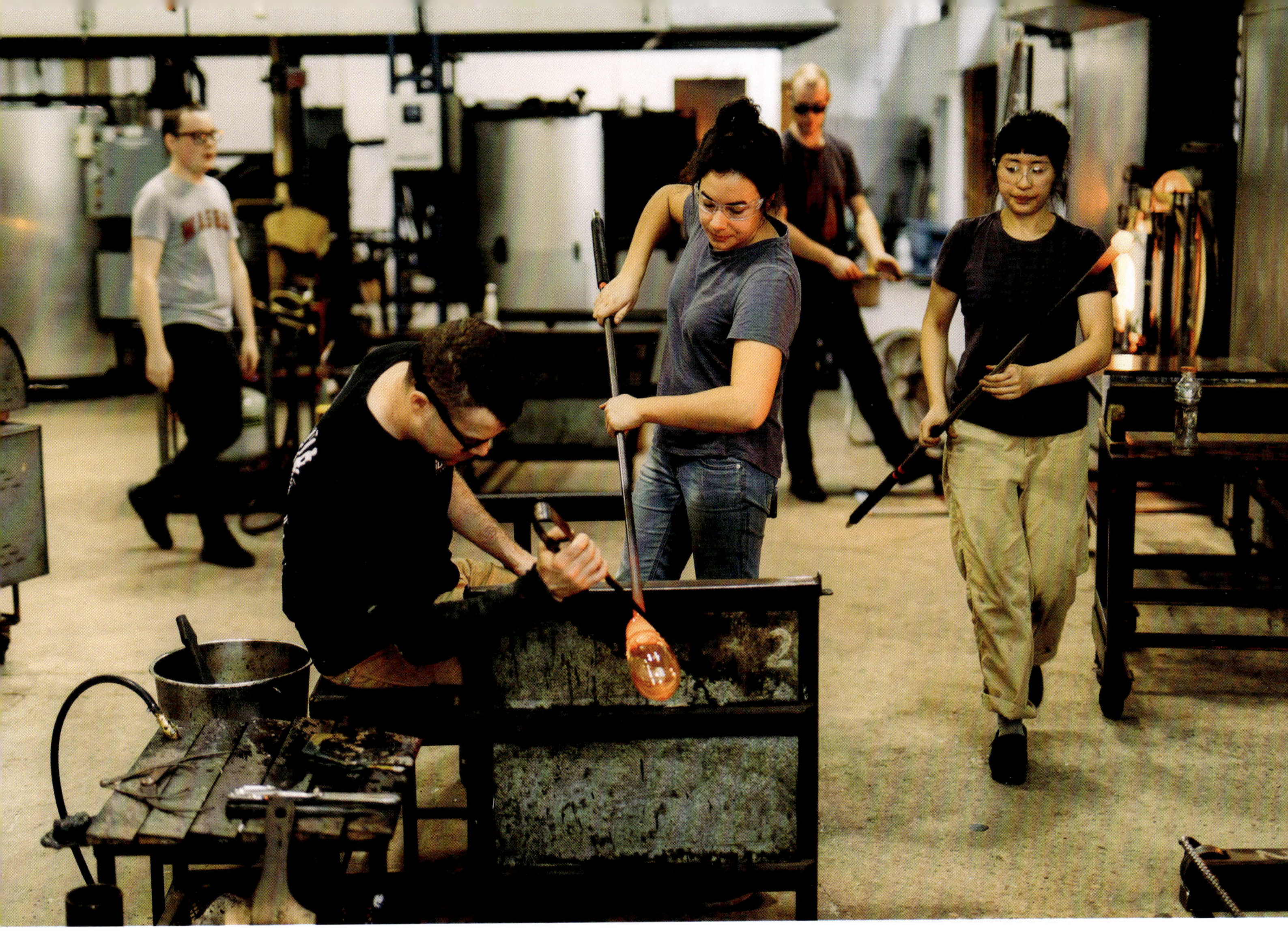

Kristel Britcher. It has also attracted many accomplished artists from around the world to undertake post-graduate study. The program is now led by acclaimed artist and JamFactory alumnus Gabriella Bisetto, who has taught at the University since 2002 and whose solo exhibition *first breath, last breath, everything in between* (26 September – 24 November), is being is being shown at JamFactory in conjunction with *Chihuly in the Botanic Garden.*

Arguably the most influential, and certainly the largest and most comprehensive educational centre in the world for artists working with glass, is the Pilchuck Glass School, co-founded by Dale Chihuly in 1971, about 80 kilometers north of Seattle. Pilchuck offers intensive one-to-two-week residential sessions from April to September each year. Over decades, many South Australian artists have attended classes as students, teaching assistants or teachers and since 2000, JamFactory has regularly sent participants in its training program to attend classes at Pilchuck through what is now a philanthropically supported annual scholarship.

The Pilchuck Glass School has provided a backdrop for many deep connections between glass artists from South Australia and those from the Pacific Northwest. Leading local artists such as Clare Belfrage, Giles Bettison, Tim Edwards, Liam Fleming and Tom Moore are among many who have taught or assisted at Pilchuck. Many have undertaken residencies at the Museum of Glass, Tacoma, just south of Seattle. Others have shown regularly with prominent commercial galleries in Seattle, including Belfrage and Edwards whose work was showcased at the prestigious Traver Gallery. The enduring glass art connections between Australia and the Pacific Northwest were celebrated in 2013 through a major exhibition at the Museum of Glass, Tacoma titled *LINKS: Australian glass and the Pacific Northwest*.

The work of six South Australian studio glass artists with various links to the United States will be shown in conjunction with *Chihuly in the Botanic Garden* in an exhibition called *Gathering Light* at JamFactory (6 December 2024 – 30 March 2025). It is also somehow fitting that this exhibition will be shown in the same gallery spaces where Chihuly's works were last exhibited in Adelaide, a quarter of a century ago.

Brian Parkes

CEO and Artistic Director, JamFactory

JamFactory hotshop, 2020
Photo: Daniel Marks, courtesy JamFactory

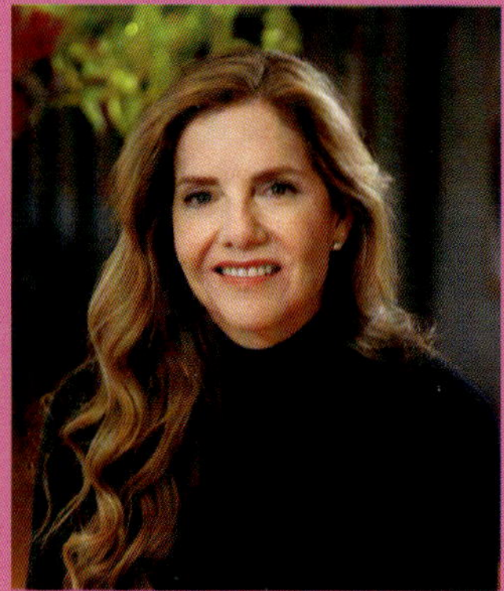
Photo: Scott Mitchell Leen

Chihuly Studio

I love to juxtapose the man-made and the natural to make people wonder and ask, "Are they man-made or did they come from nature?" That's a very important part of my work.

–Dale Chihuly

For an artist who, six decades into his career, still experiments and evolves, Dale Chihuly's inspirations have remained remarkably consistent. The fluidity of molten glass itself captivates him, of course, but it's the organic and unrestrained shapes found in nature–flowers, seagrass, vines, shells, cacti, grasses–that provide an endless vocabulary of forms with which he experiments. Given his sources of inspiration, it is little wonder that since his first botanical garden exhibition in 2001, he has returned to presenting work in the conservatories and arbours of botanical gardens time and again. His affection for gardens is enormous.

It's also little wonder that Chihuly has chosen Australia for his first-ever major garden exhibition in the Southern Hemisphere. Australia has held a special place in his heart since he presented a handful of installations there throughout the 1990s, including the eleven-metre-tall *Cobalt and Clear Chandelier* at Sydney Opera House in 1998. Now in 2024, Chihuly returns with a major body of work that represents a quarter century of evolution.

Adelaide's natural beauty, vibrant arts community and historic botanic gardens make it a wonderful location for this exhibition. We are pleased and honoured to share *Chihuly in the Botanic Garden* with the people of Adelaide.

With gratitude,
Leslie Jackson Chihuly
President and CEO, Chihuly Studio

Dale Chihuly, 2017
Photo: Scott Mitchell Leen

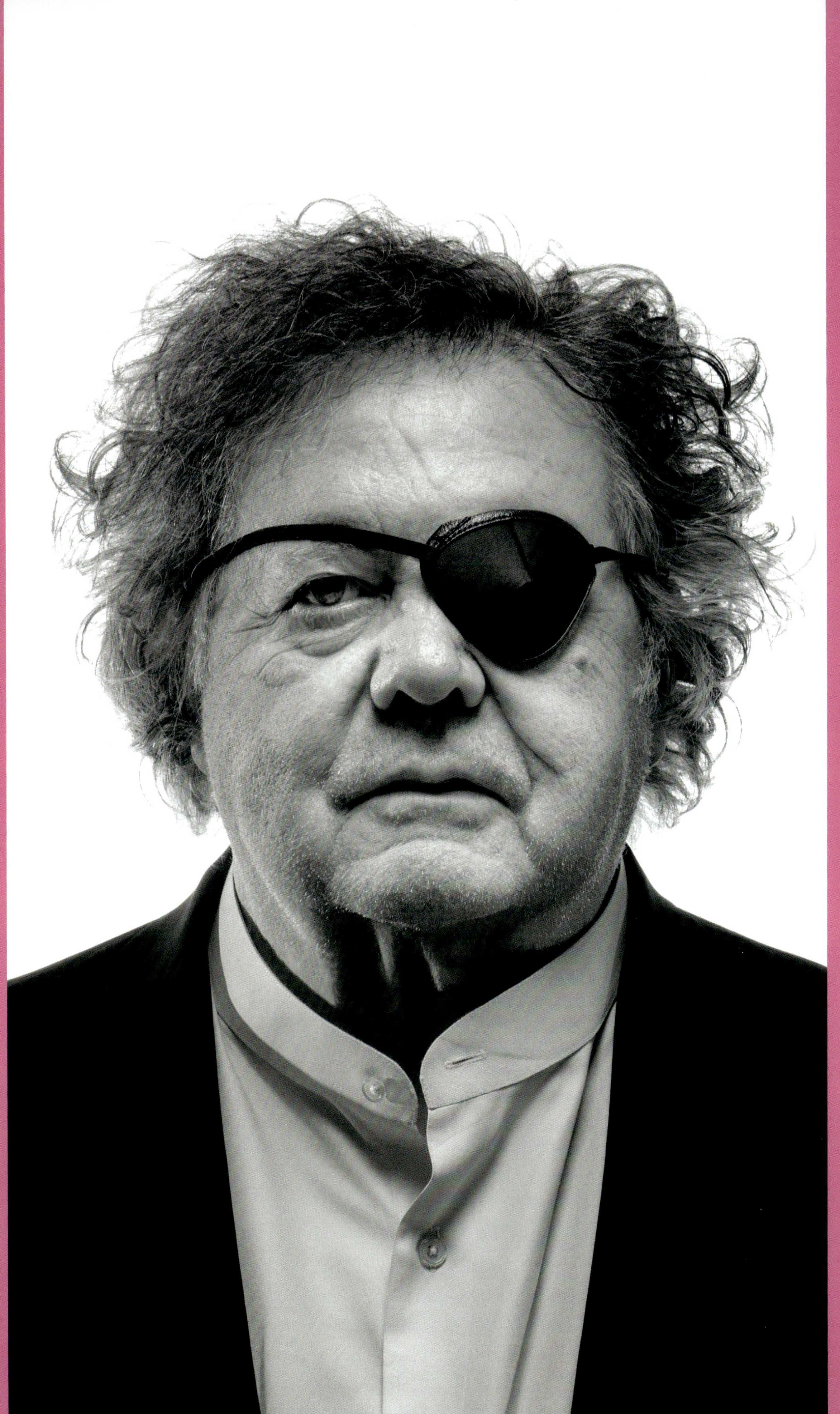

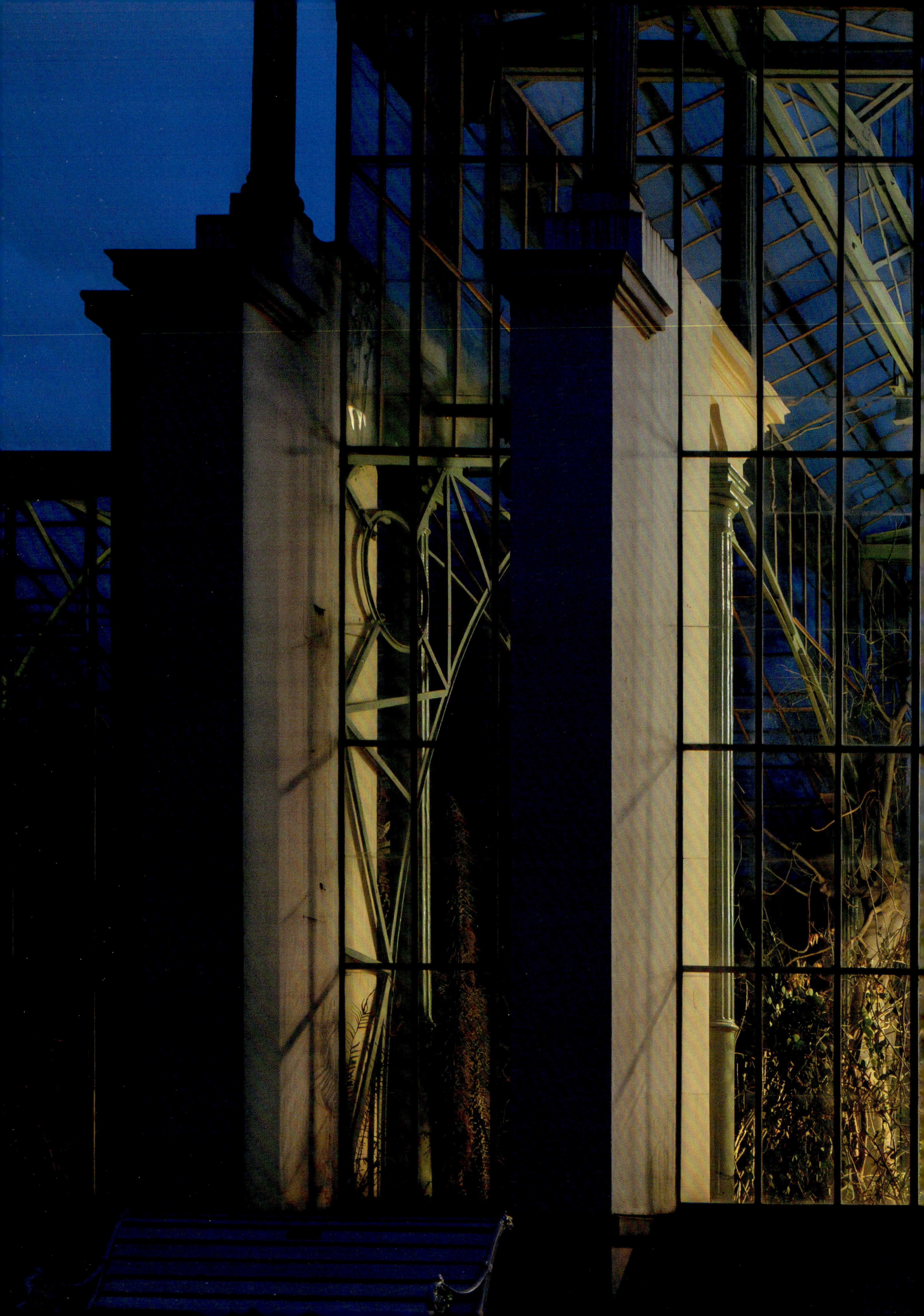

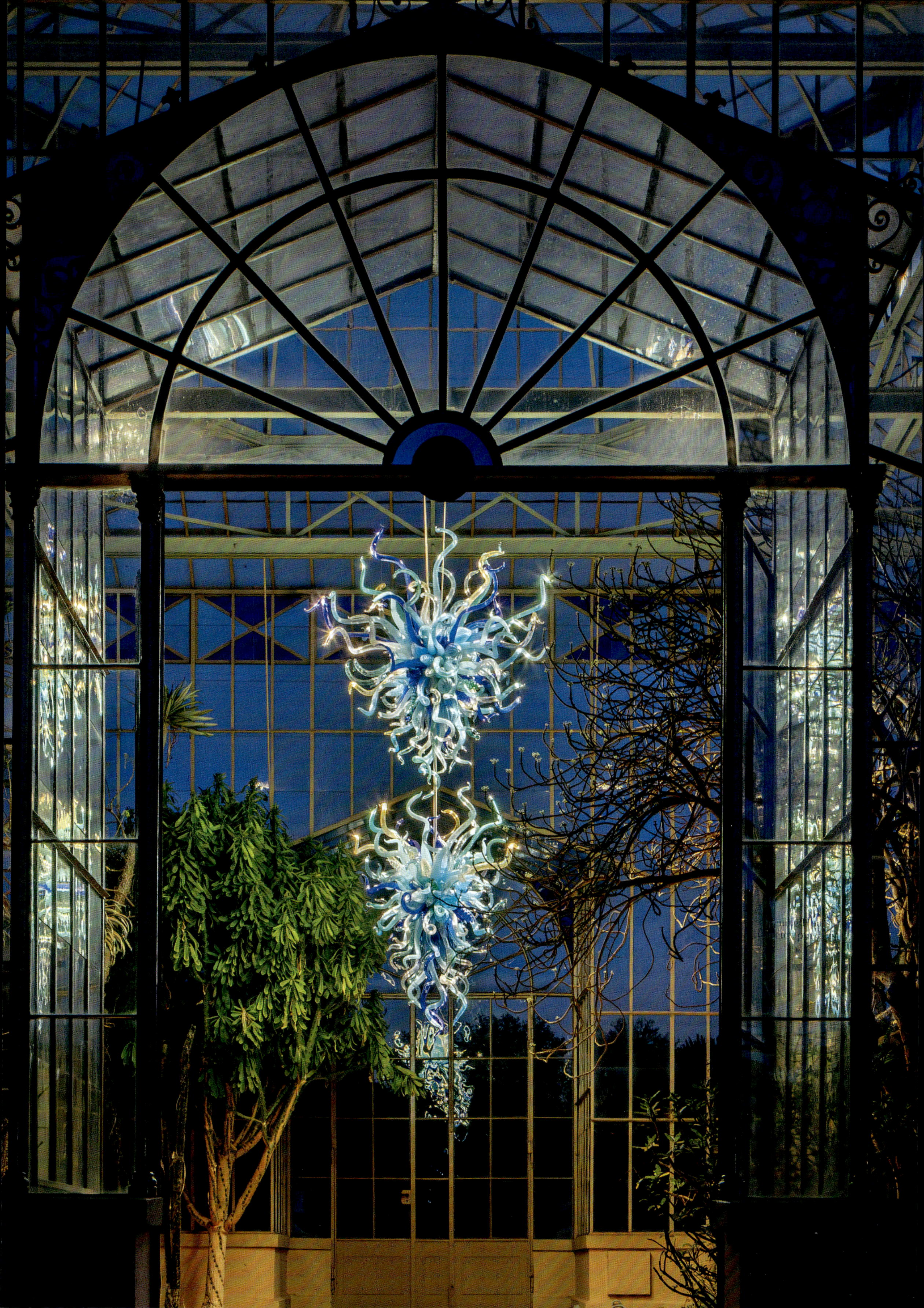

Works in the landscape

Fifteen installations of stunning, large scale glass sculptures have been carefully placed throughout the Botanic Garden, transforming as the light changes, as the foliage turns with the seasons, and as the night takes hold. Chihuly selects pieces from his diverse series that work with, celebrate and amplify the beauty of their natural surroundings.

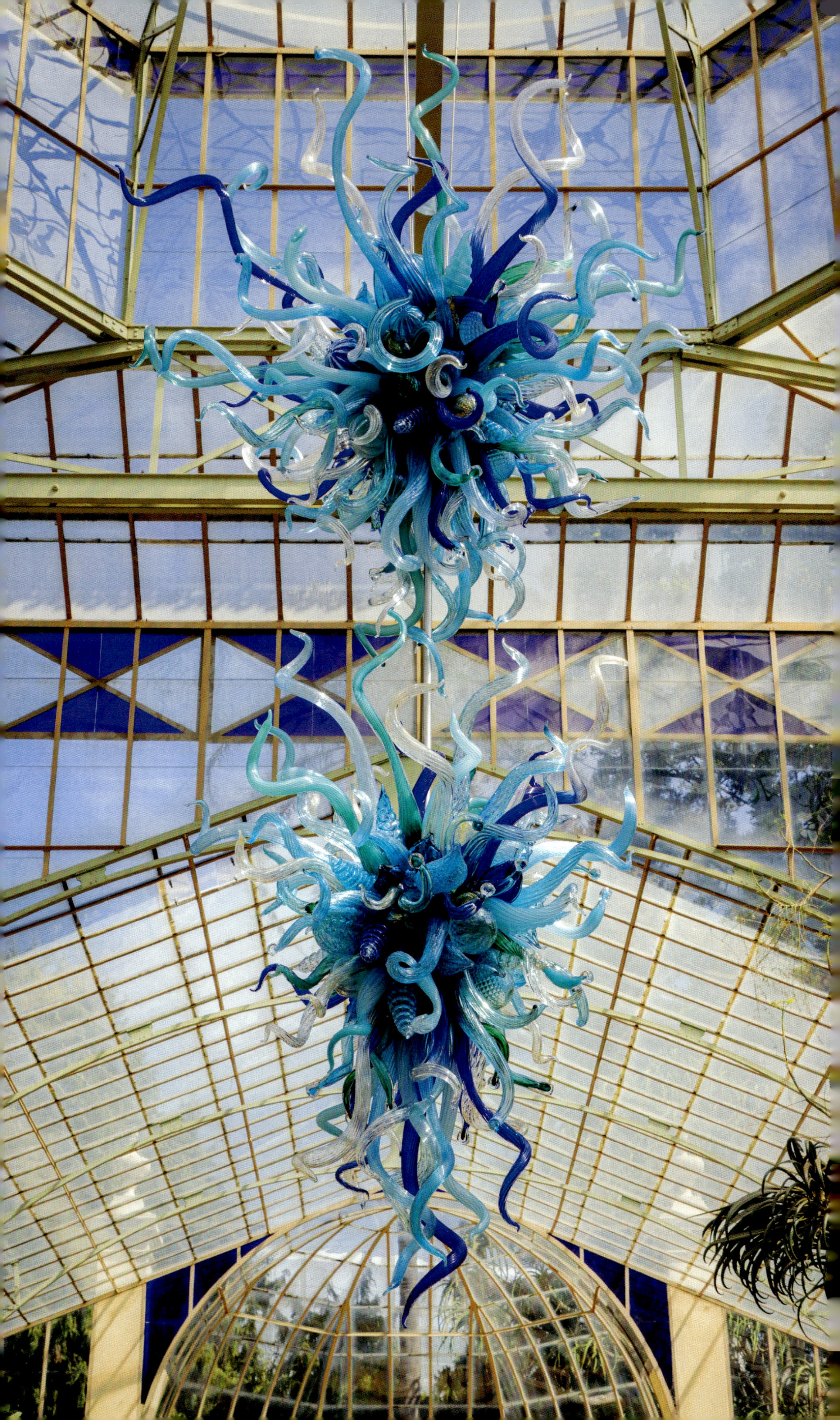

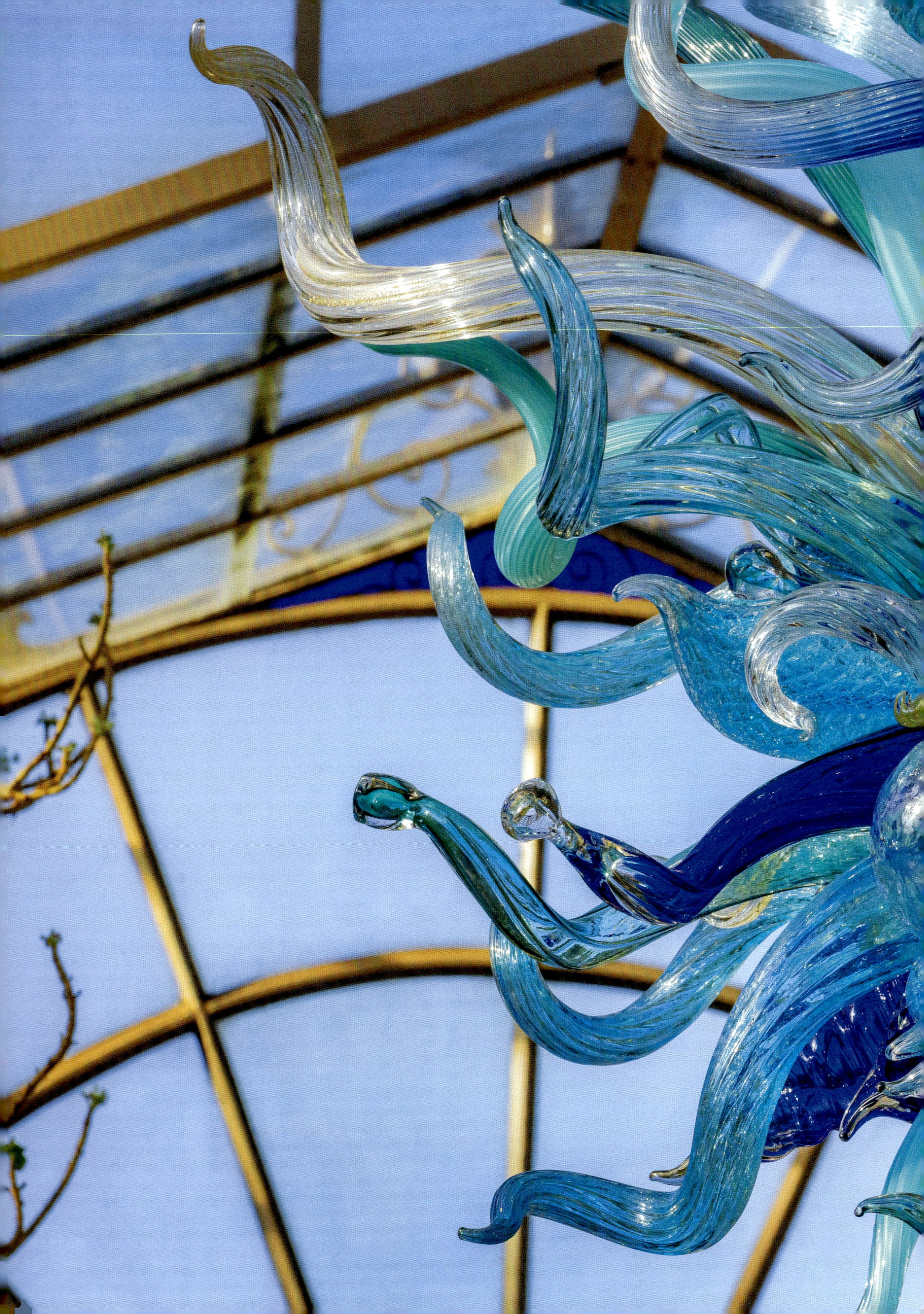

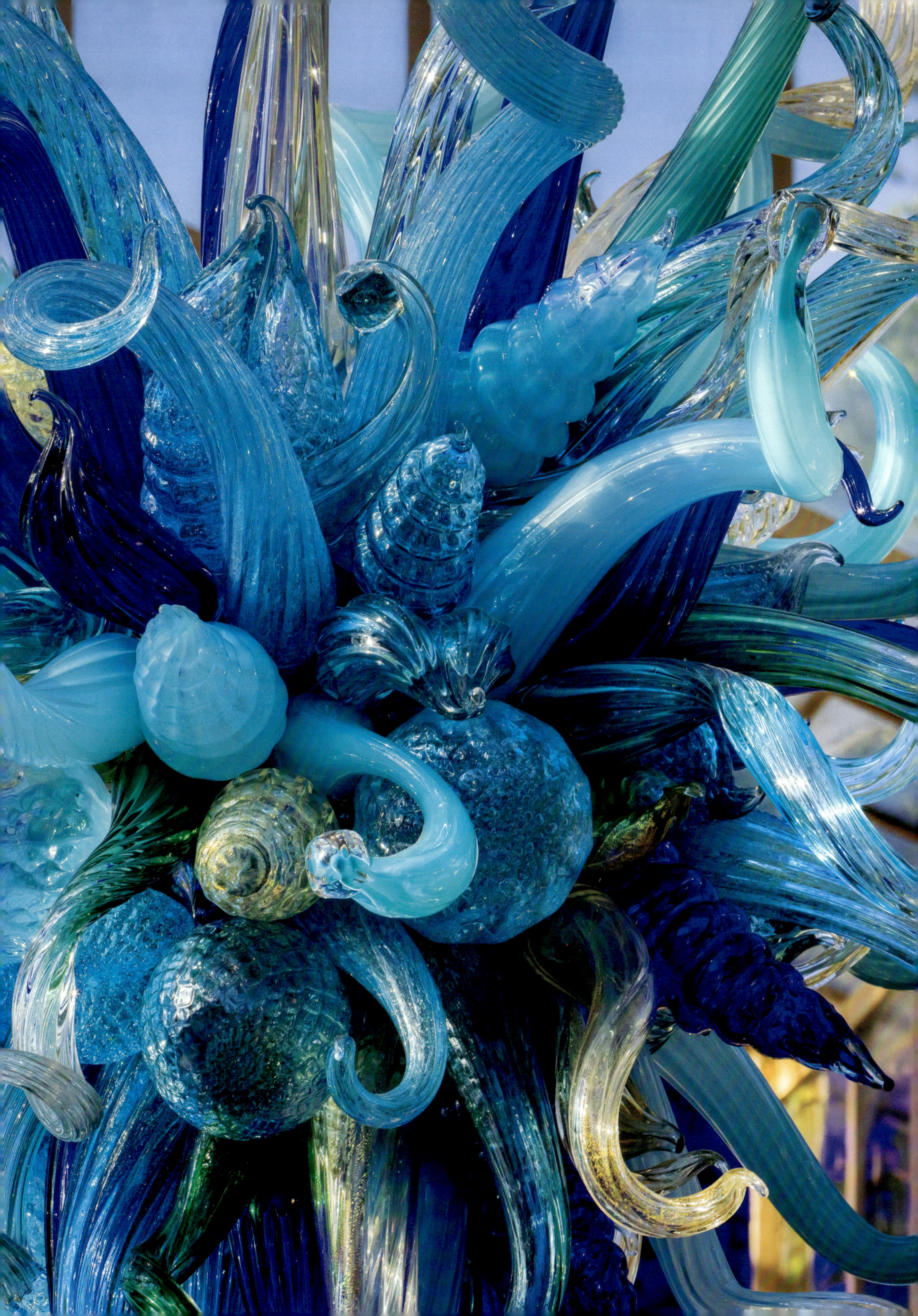

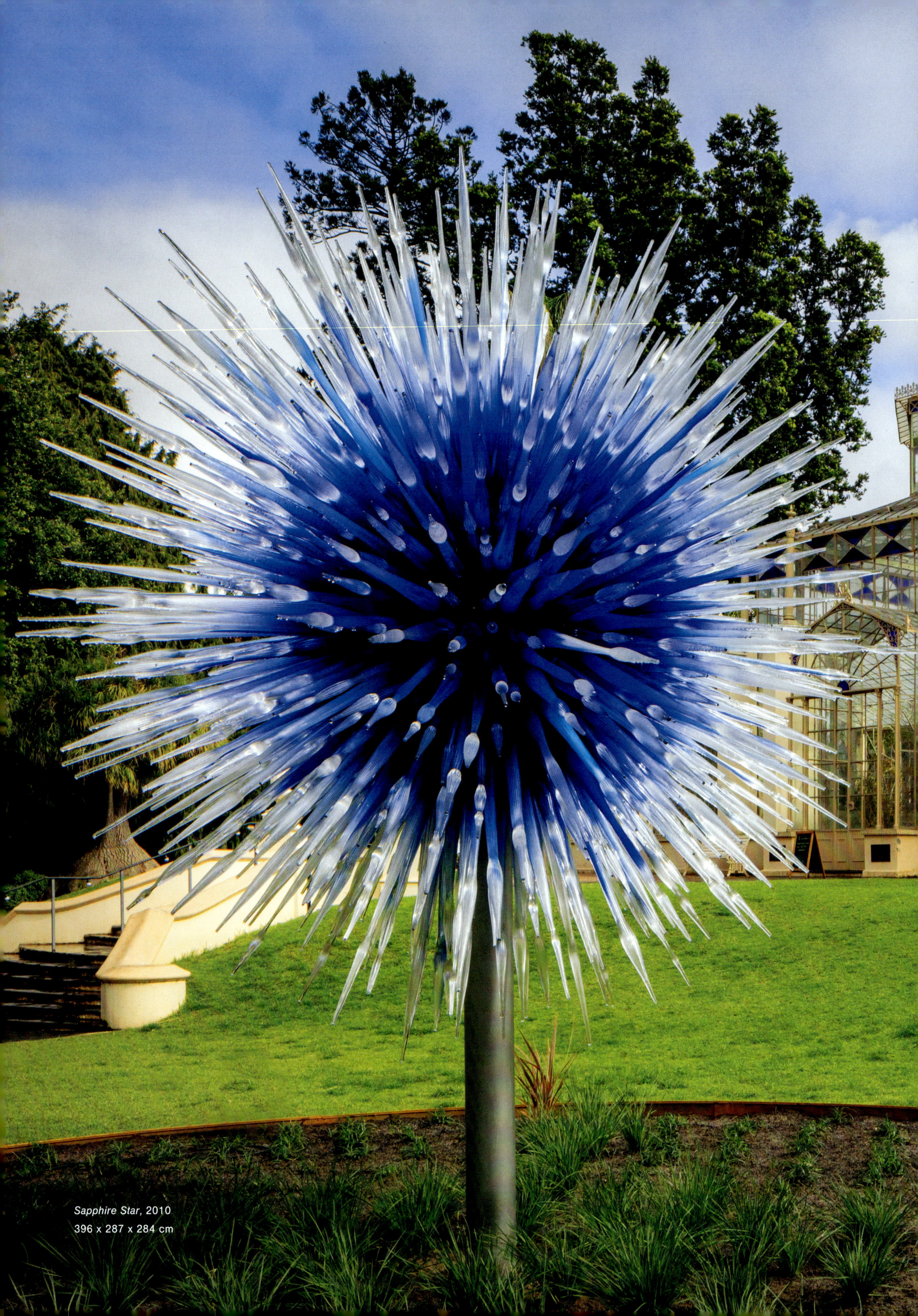

Sapphire Star, 2010
396 x 287 x 284 cm

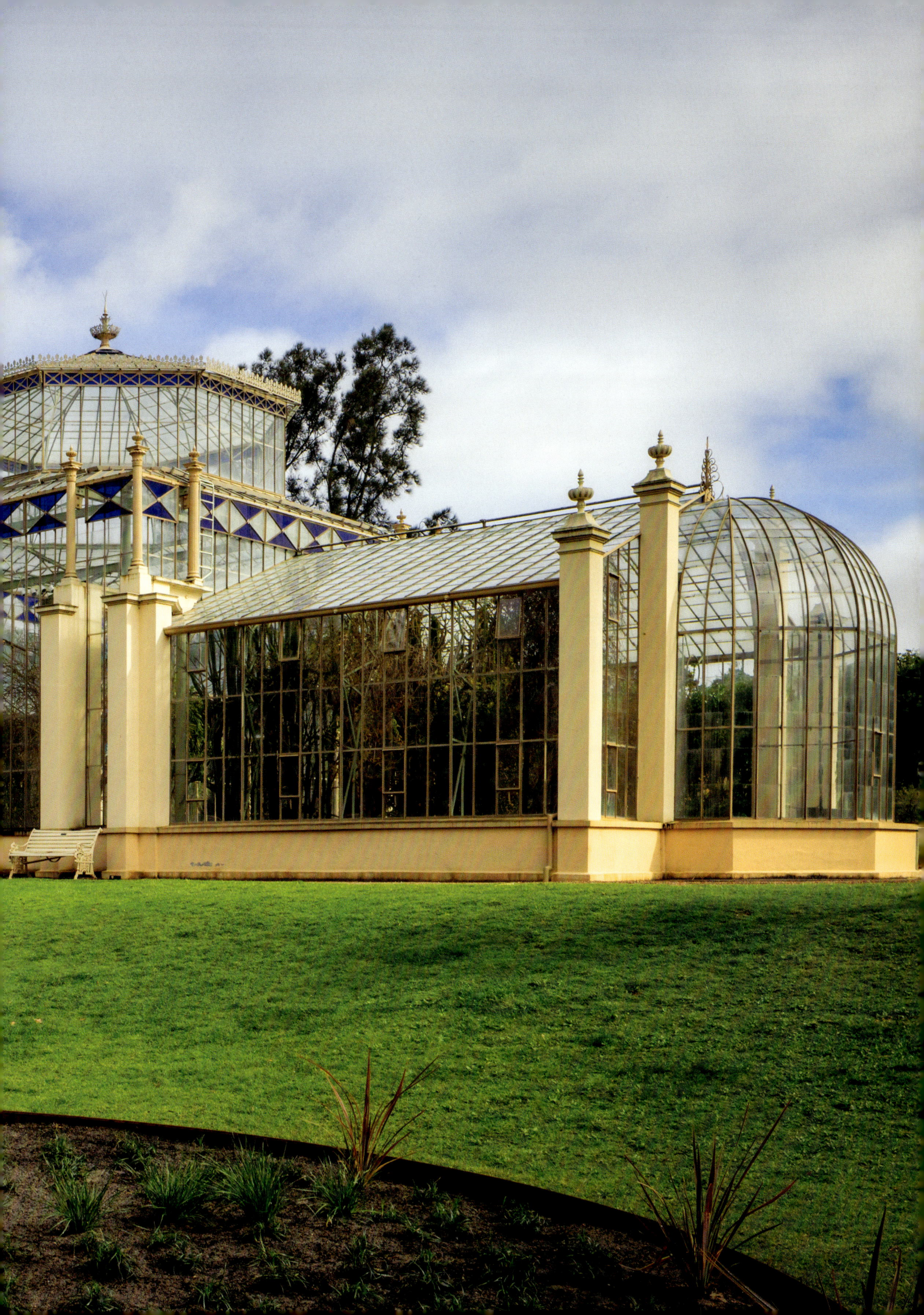

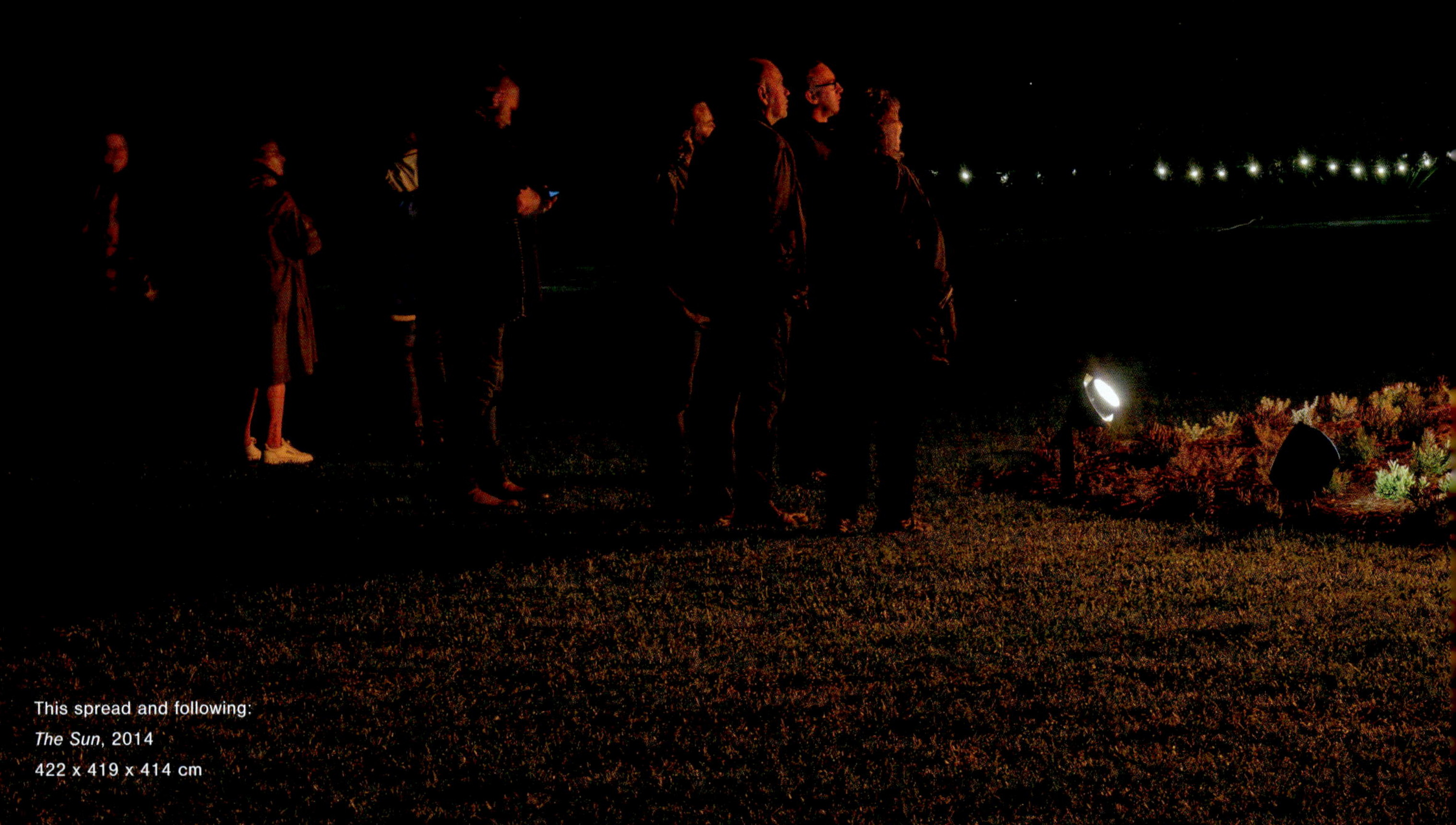

This spread and following:
The Sun, 2014
422 x 419 x 414 cm

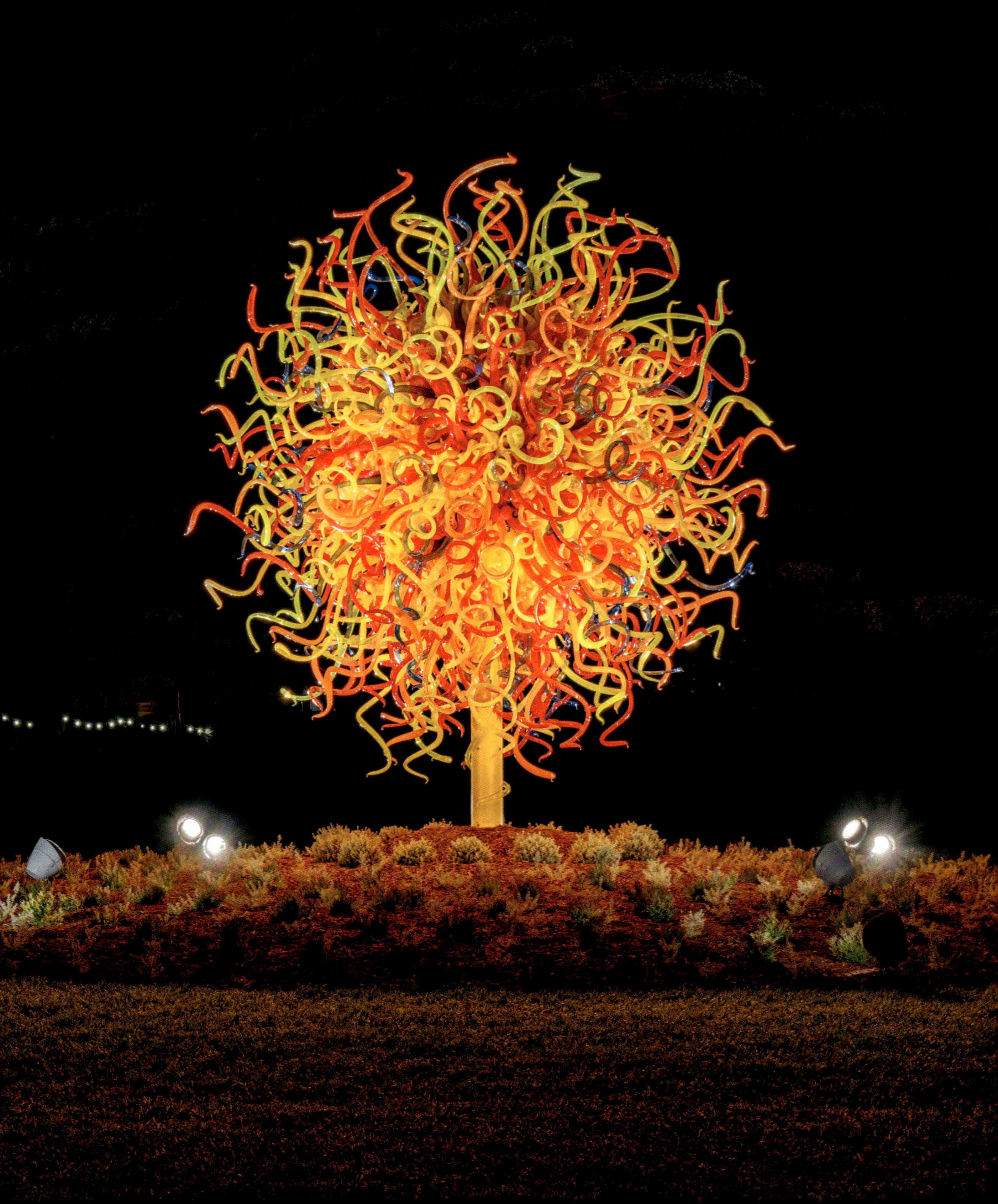

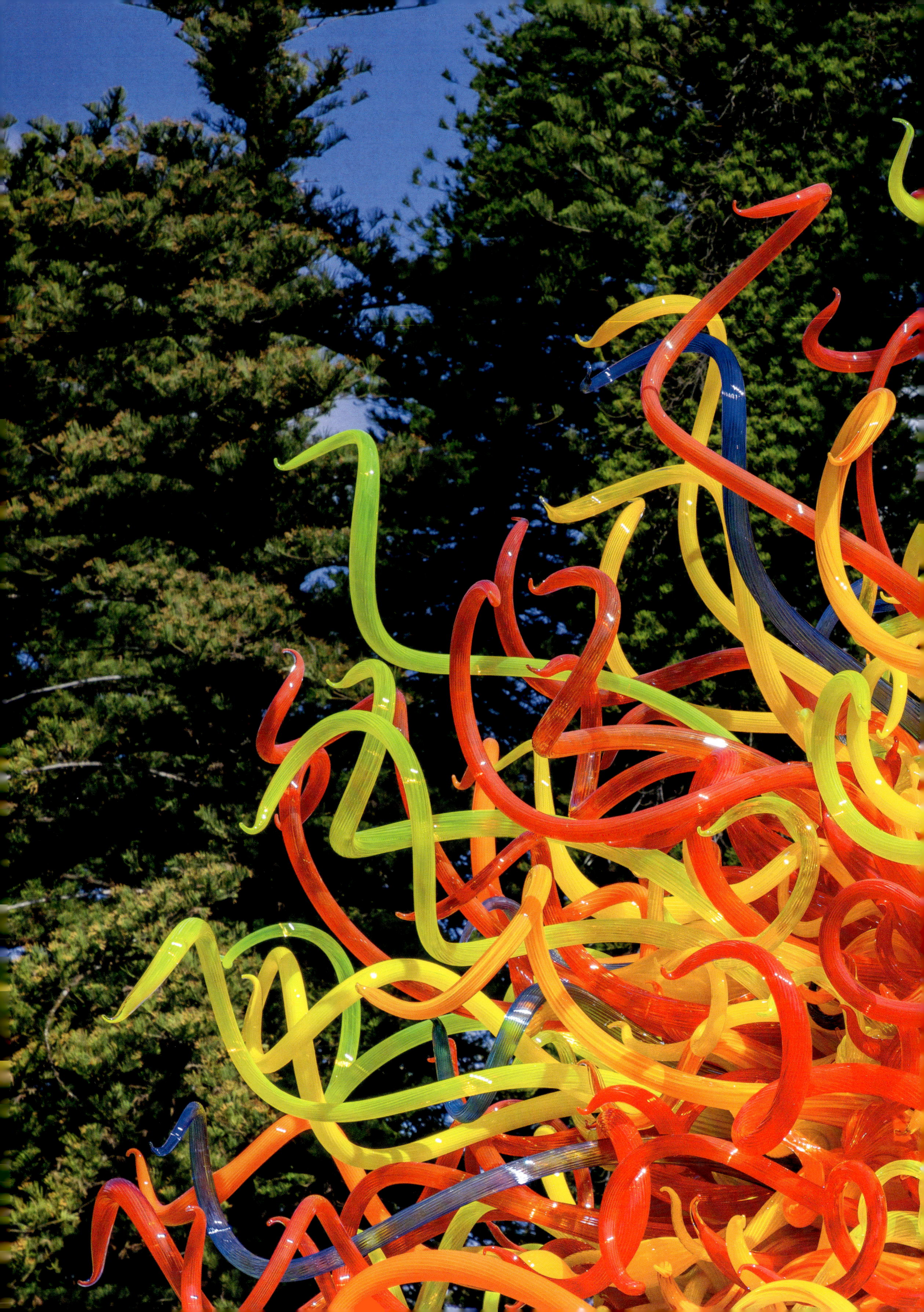

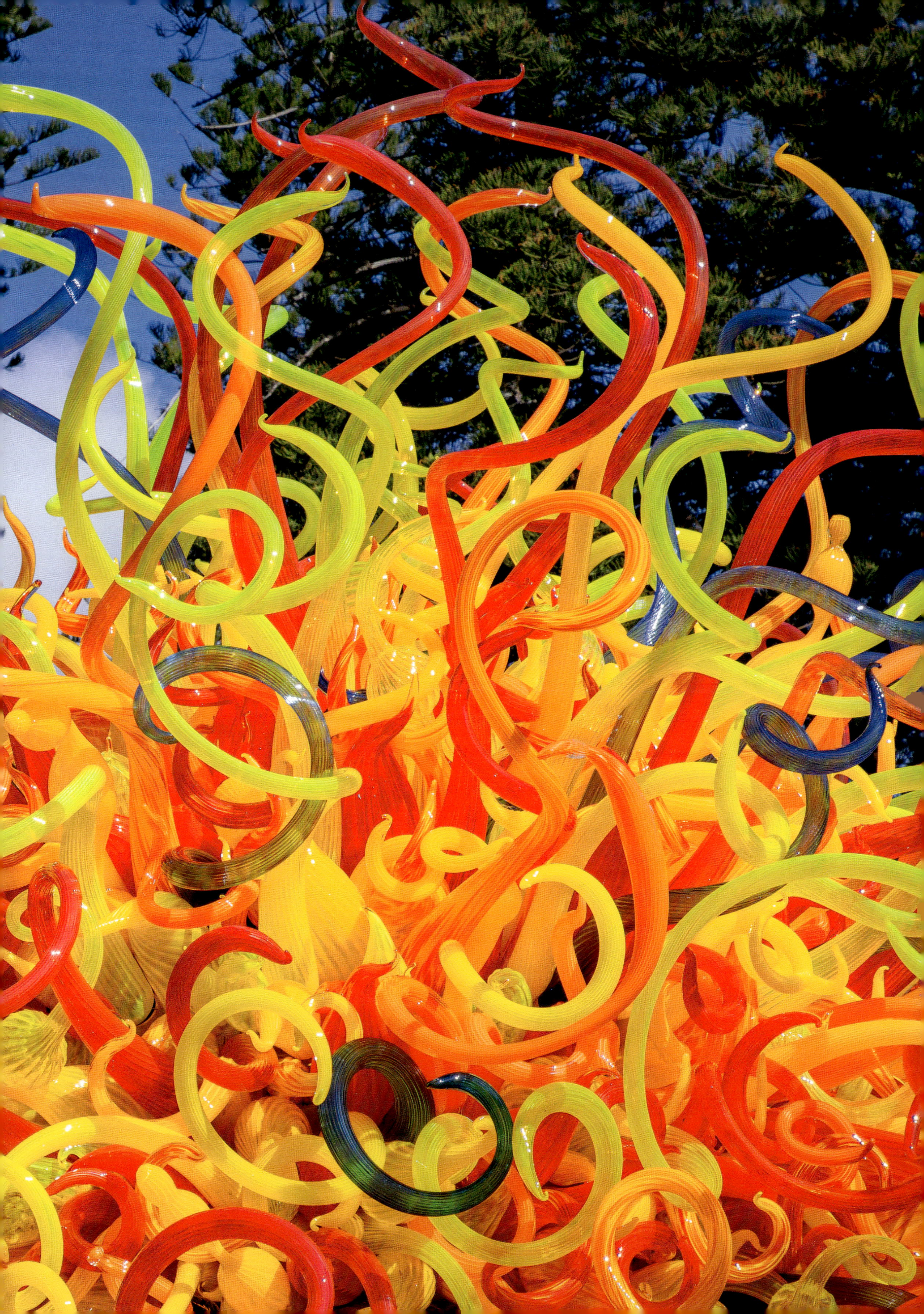

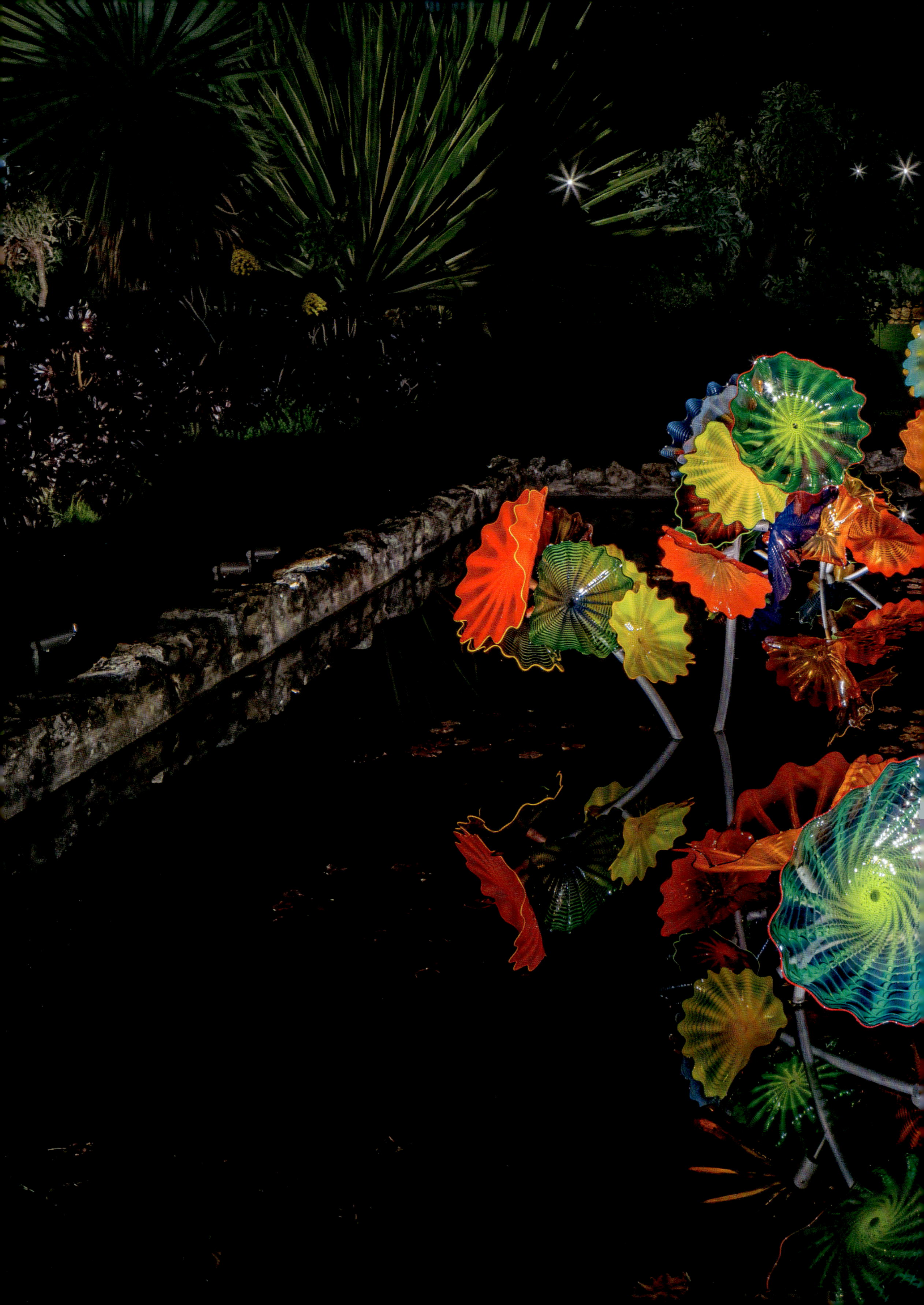

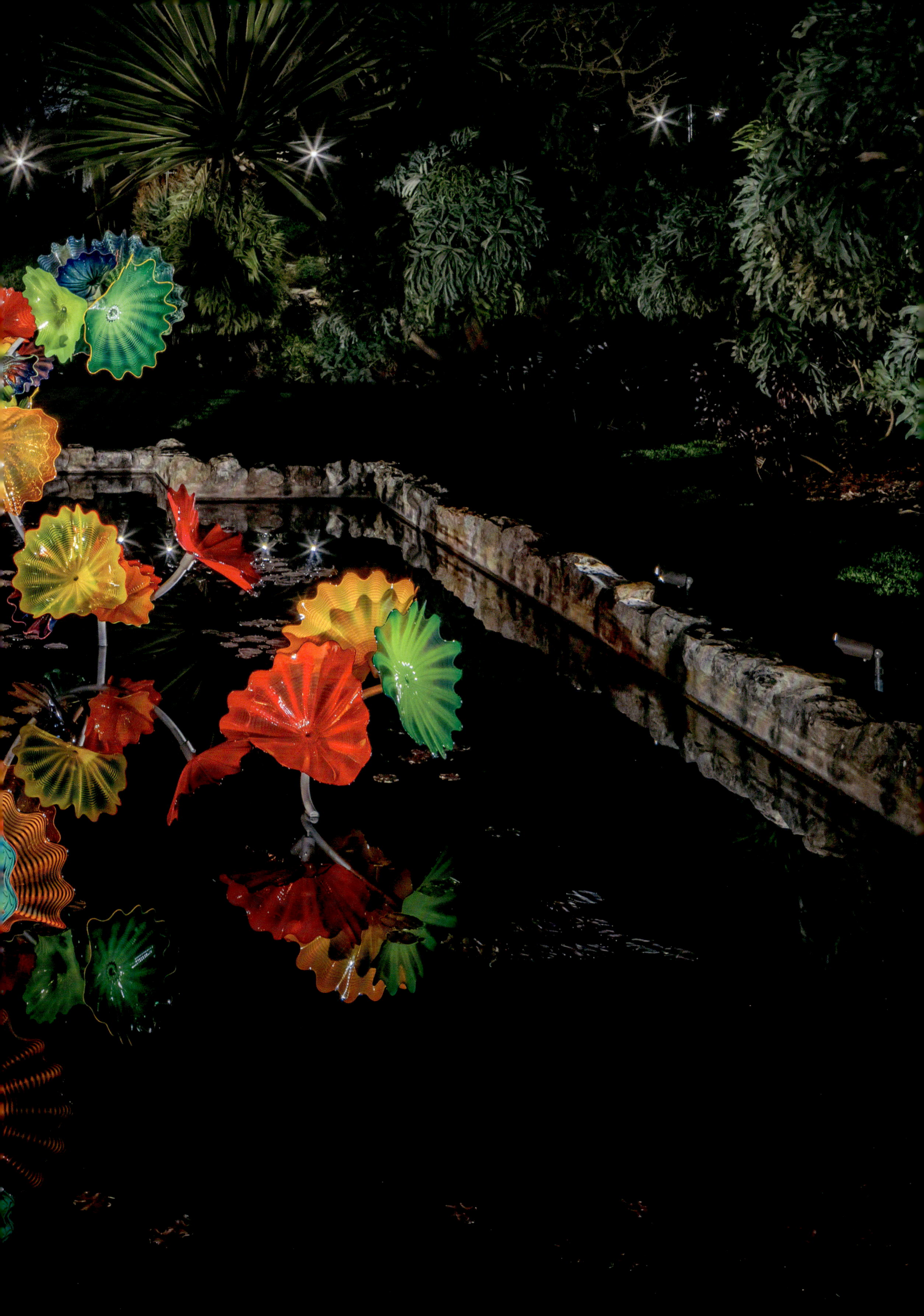

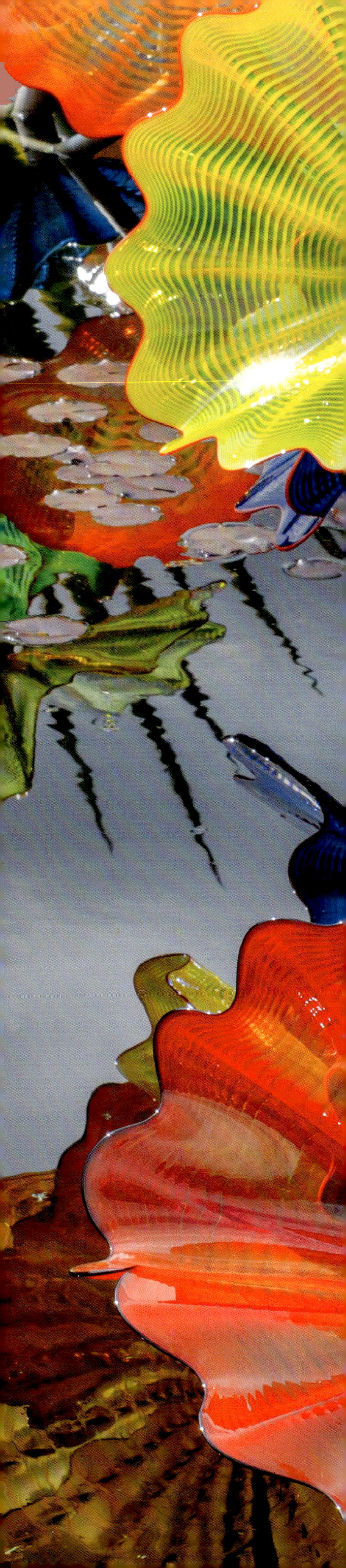

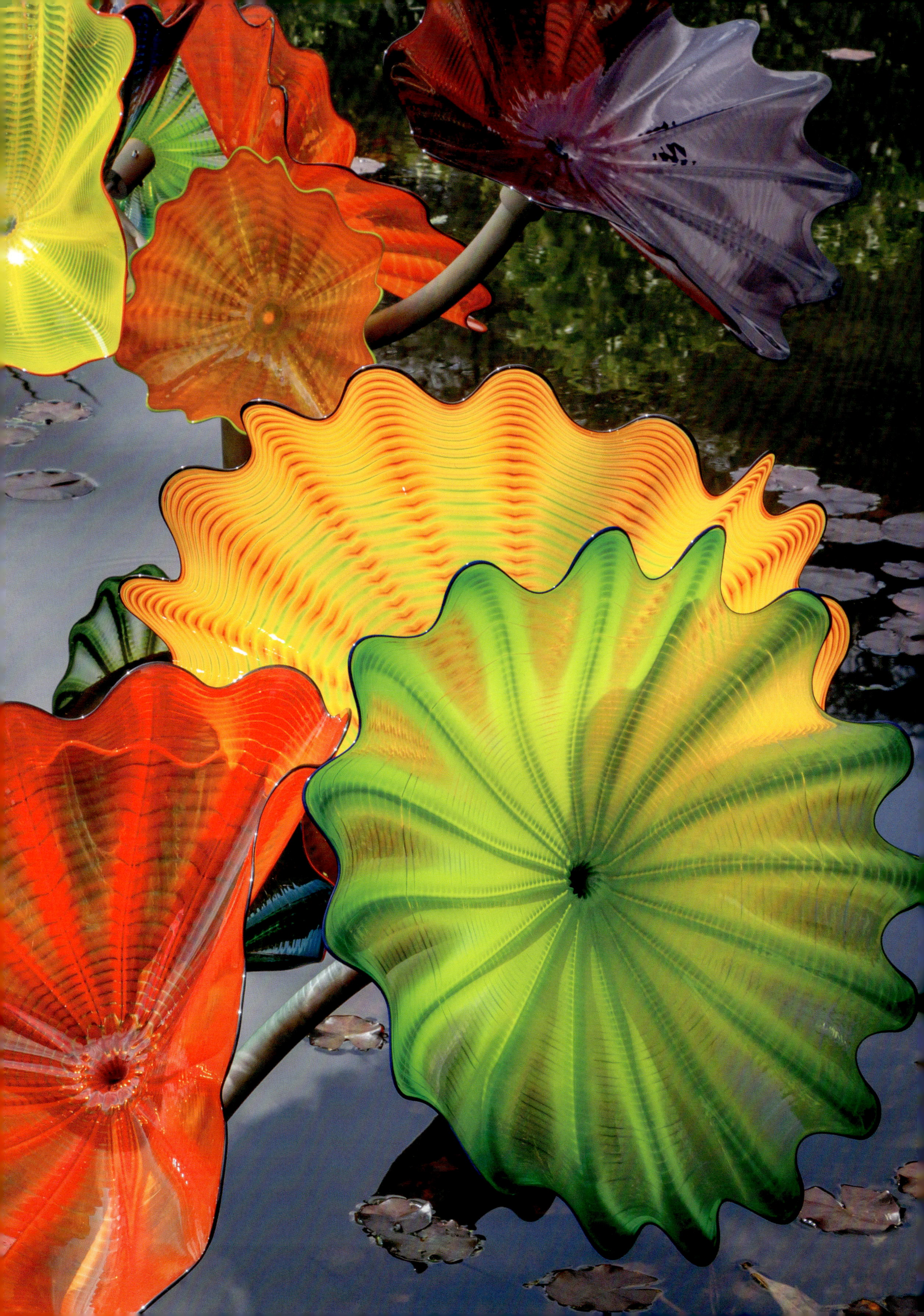

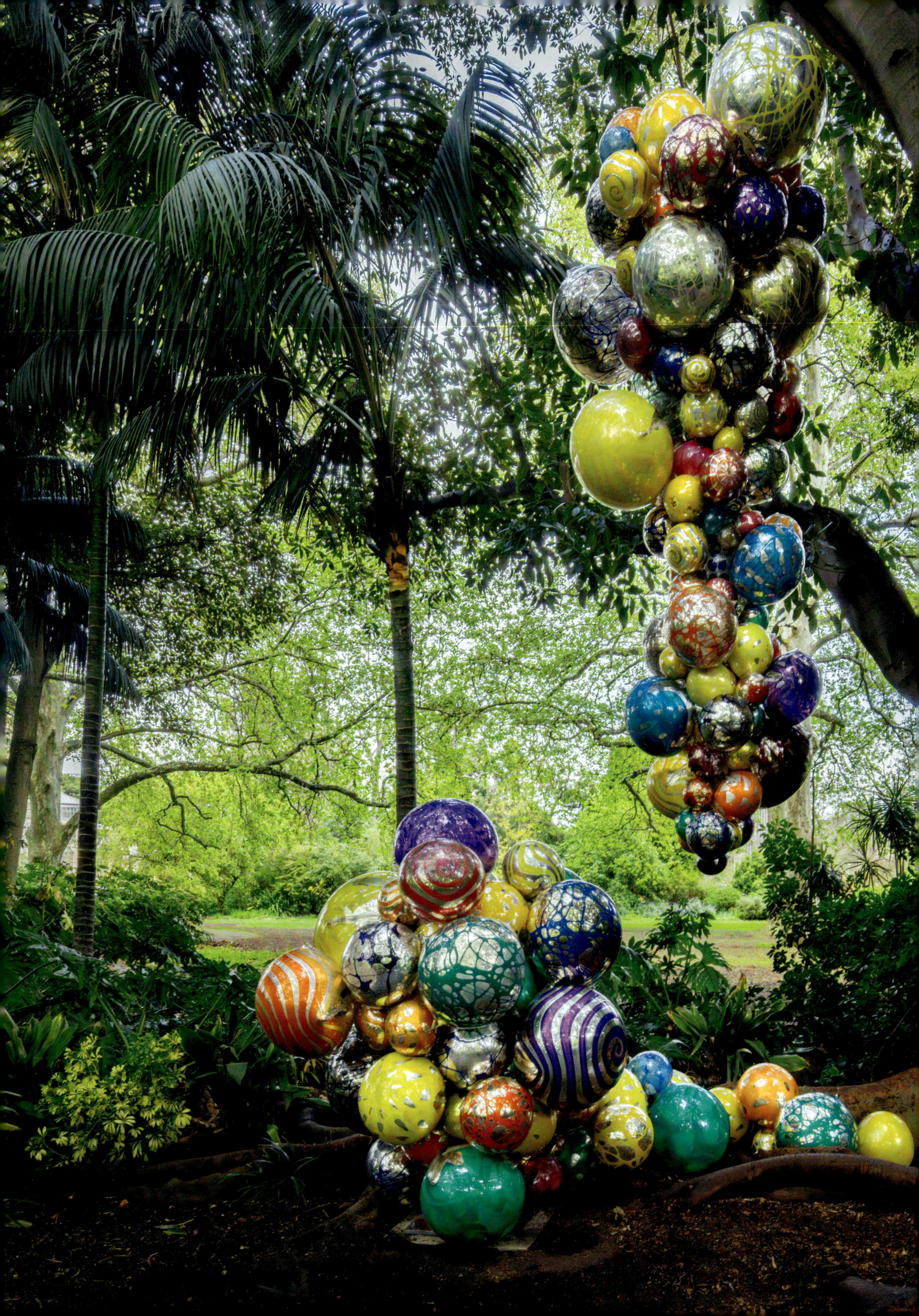

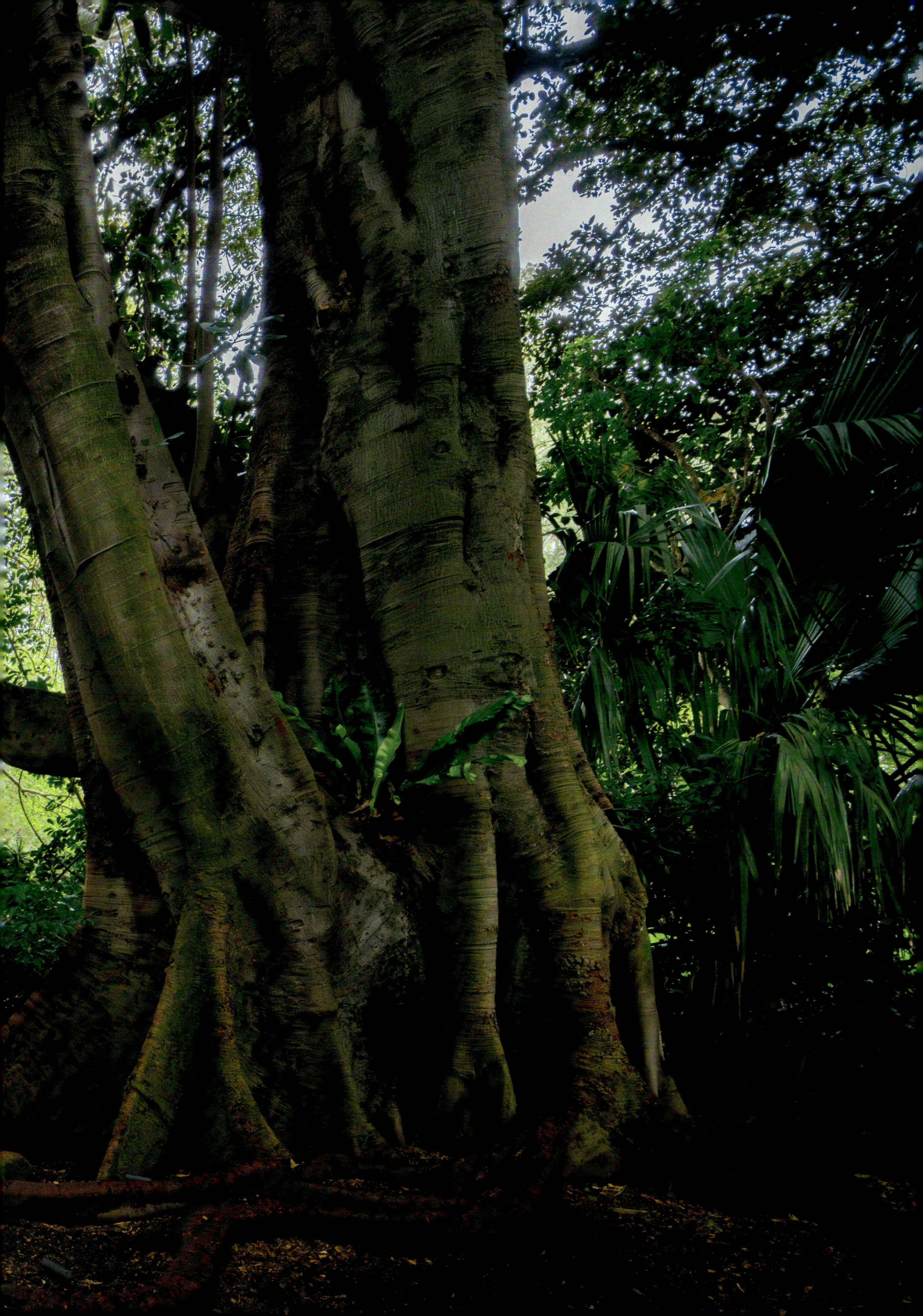

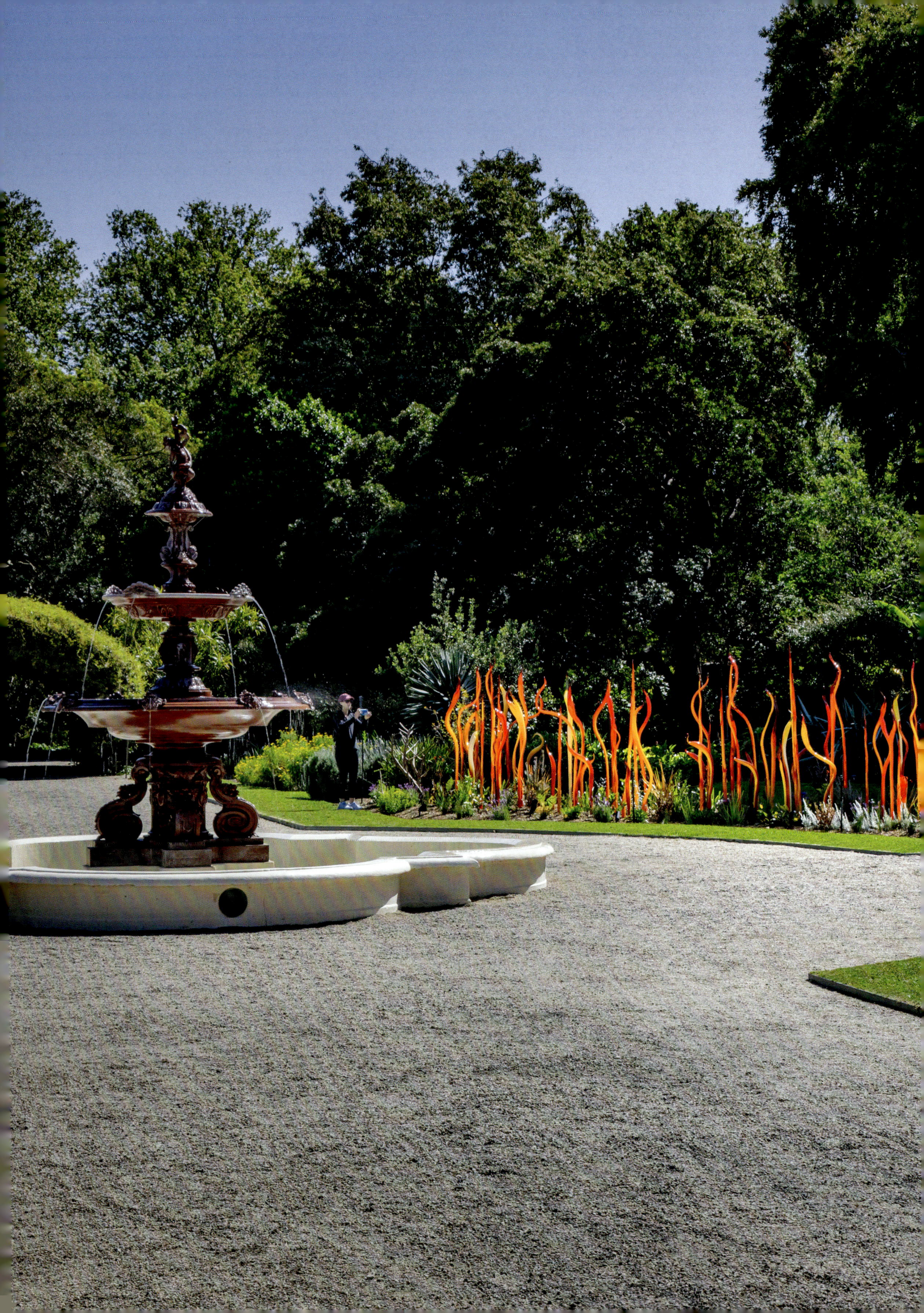

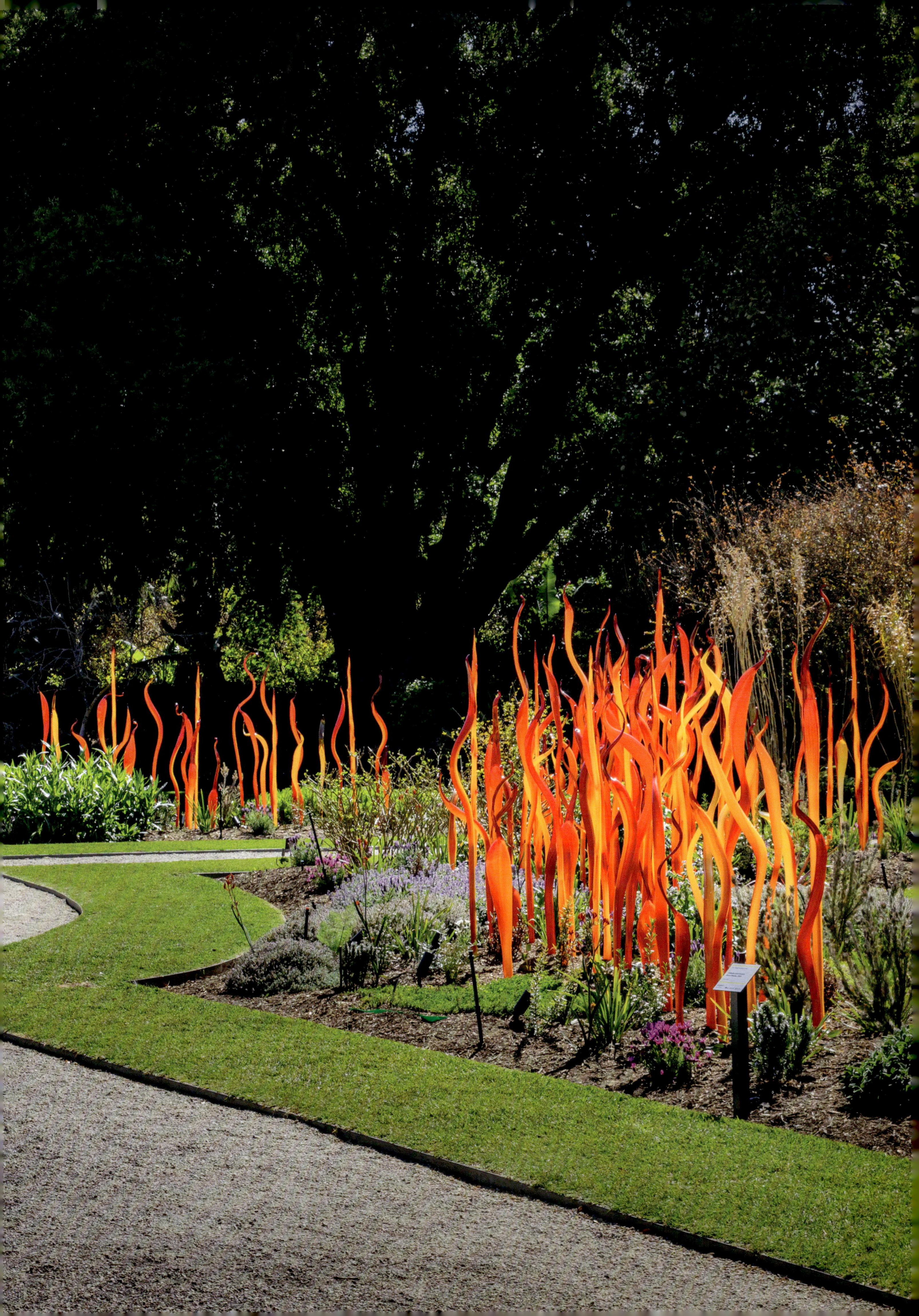

Previous and this spread:

Cattails and Copper Birch Reeds, 2024

Following spread:

Float Boat, 2019

94 x 450 x 114 cm

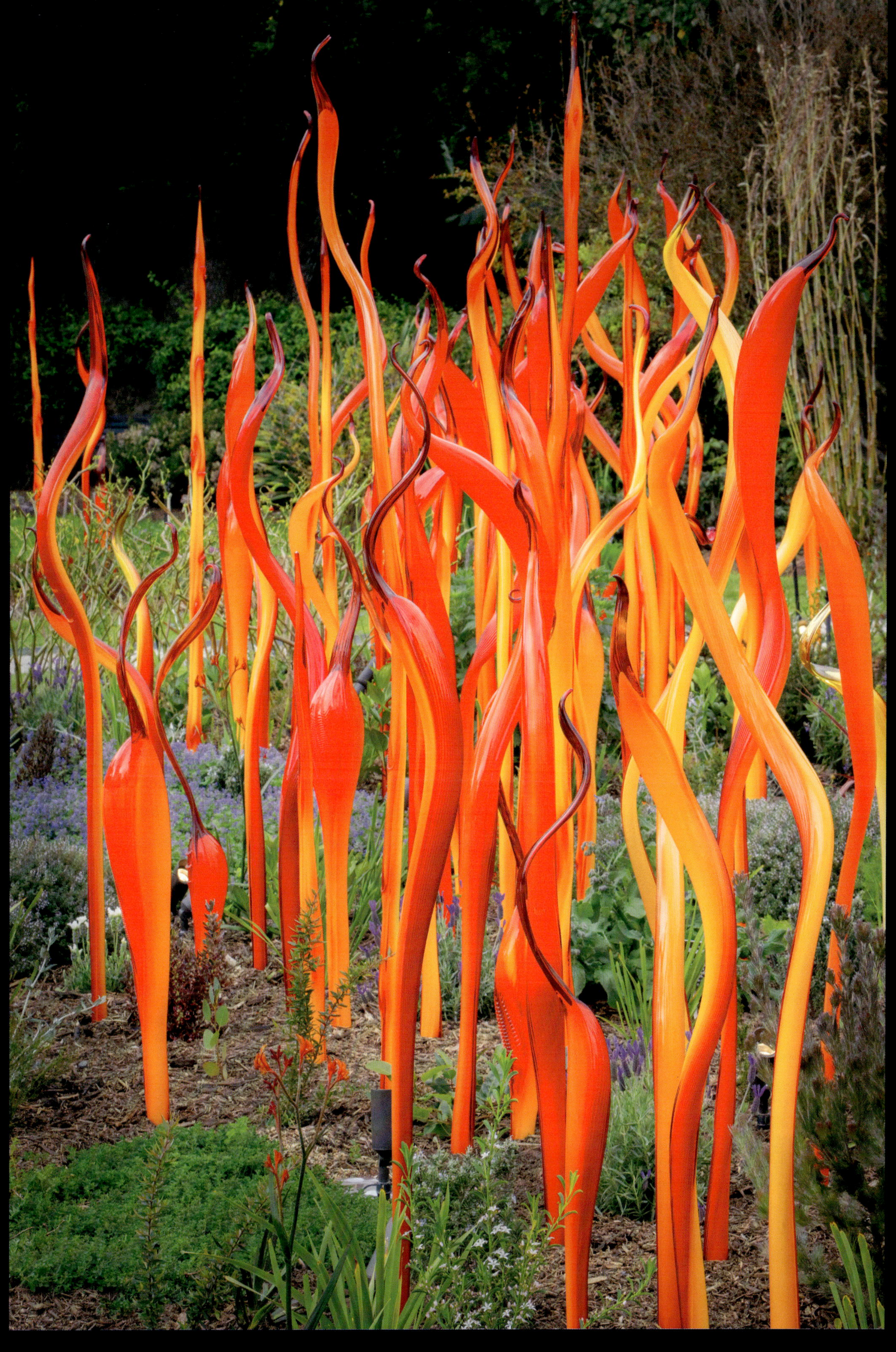

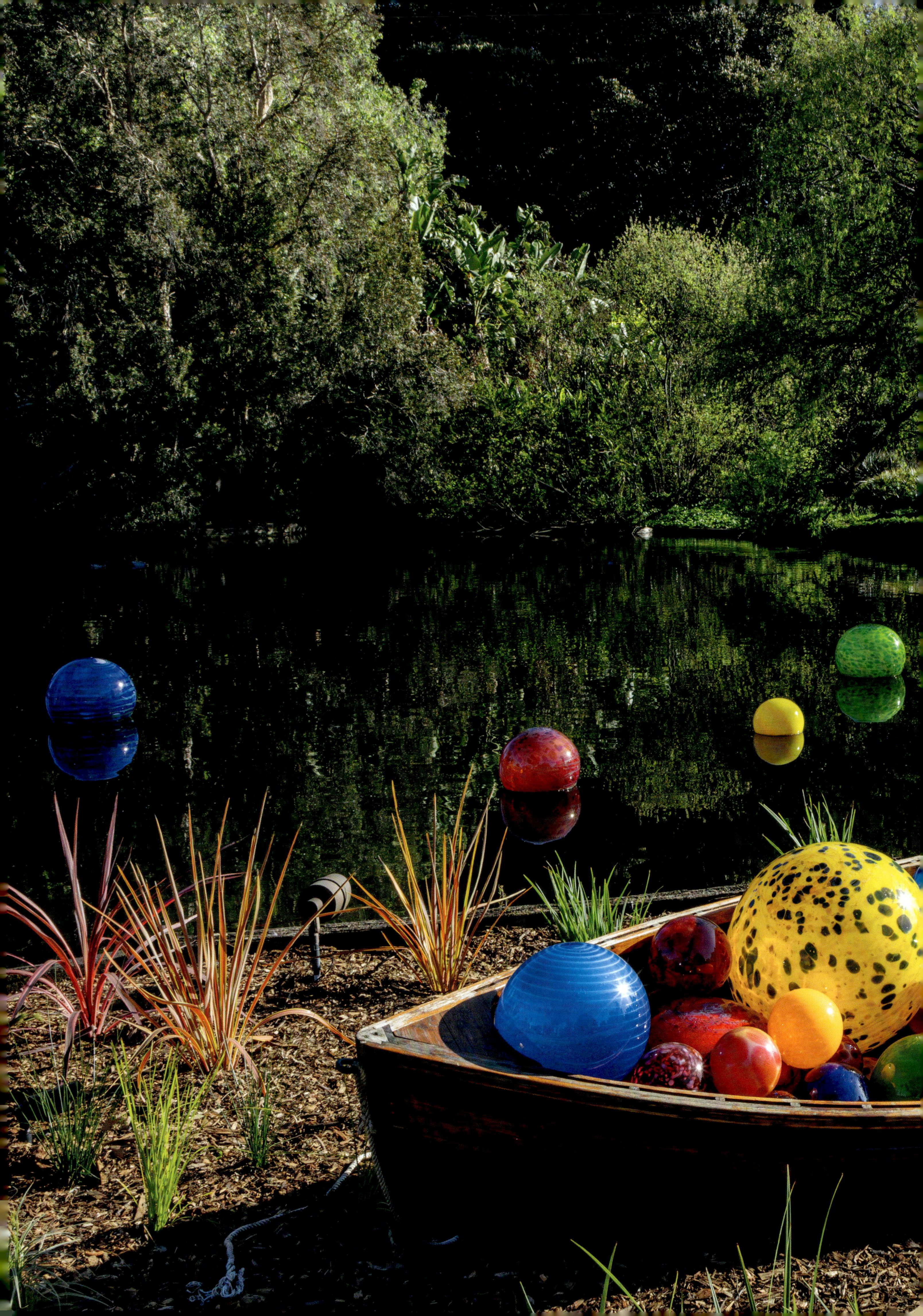

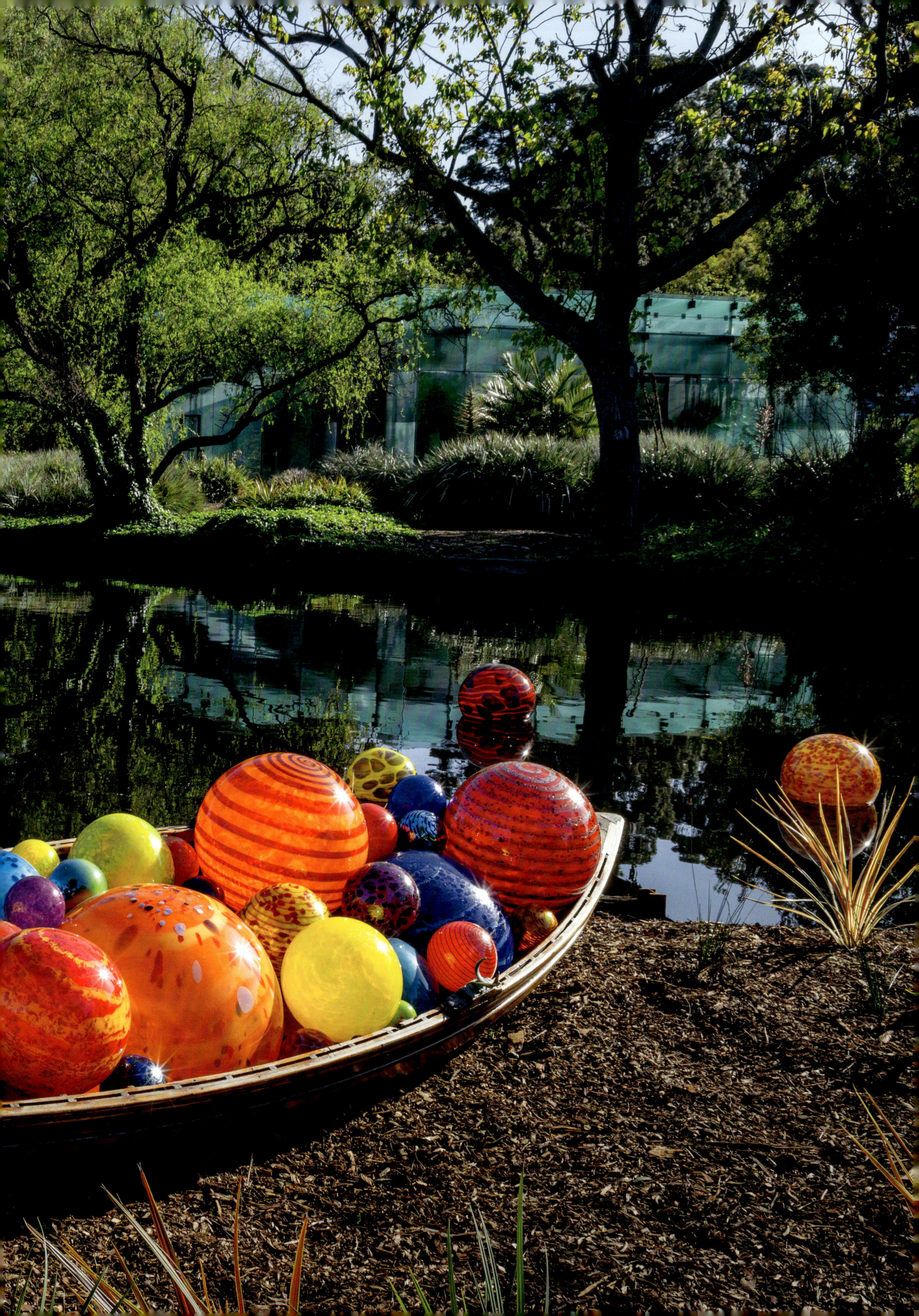

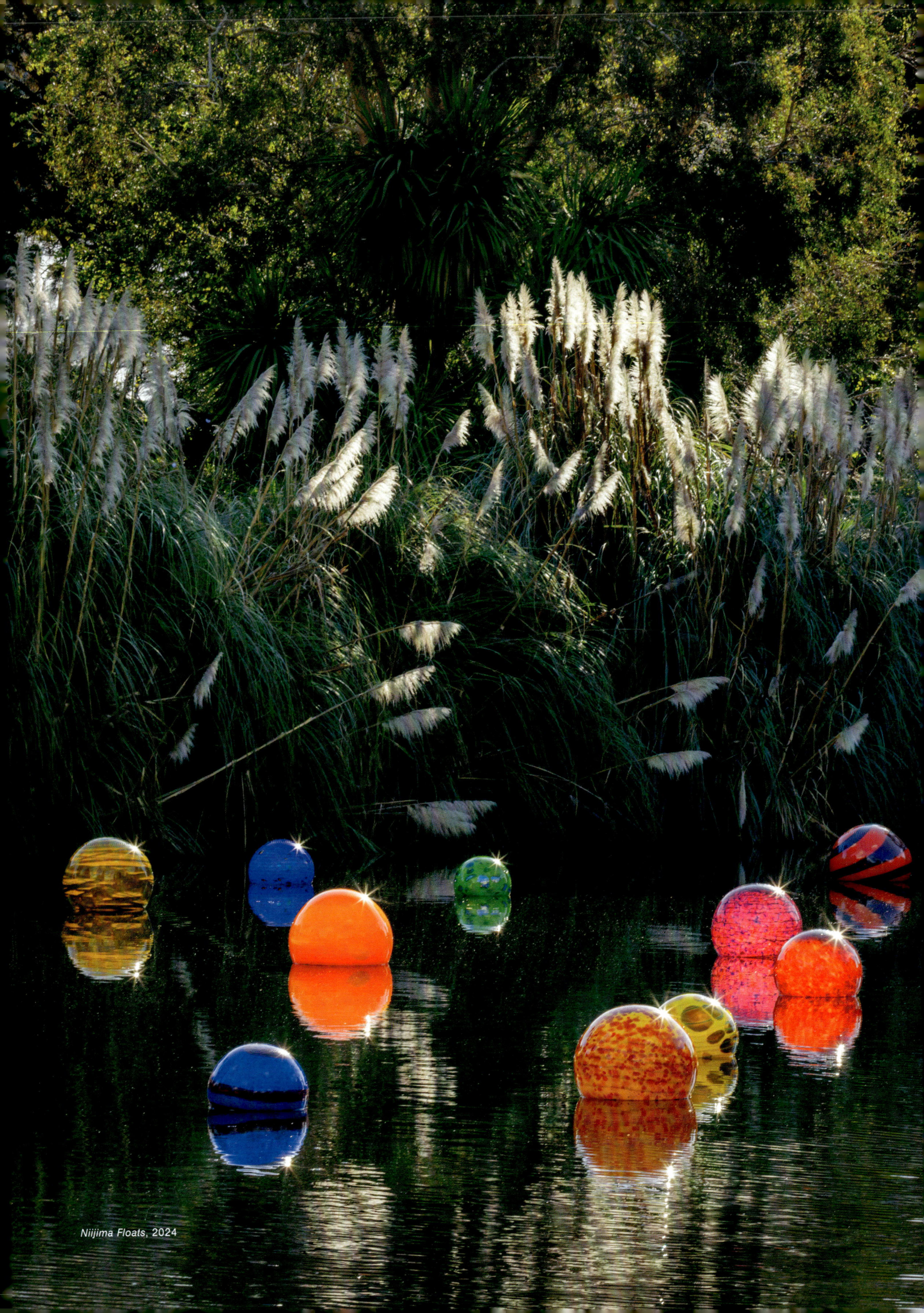

Niijima Floats, 2024

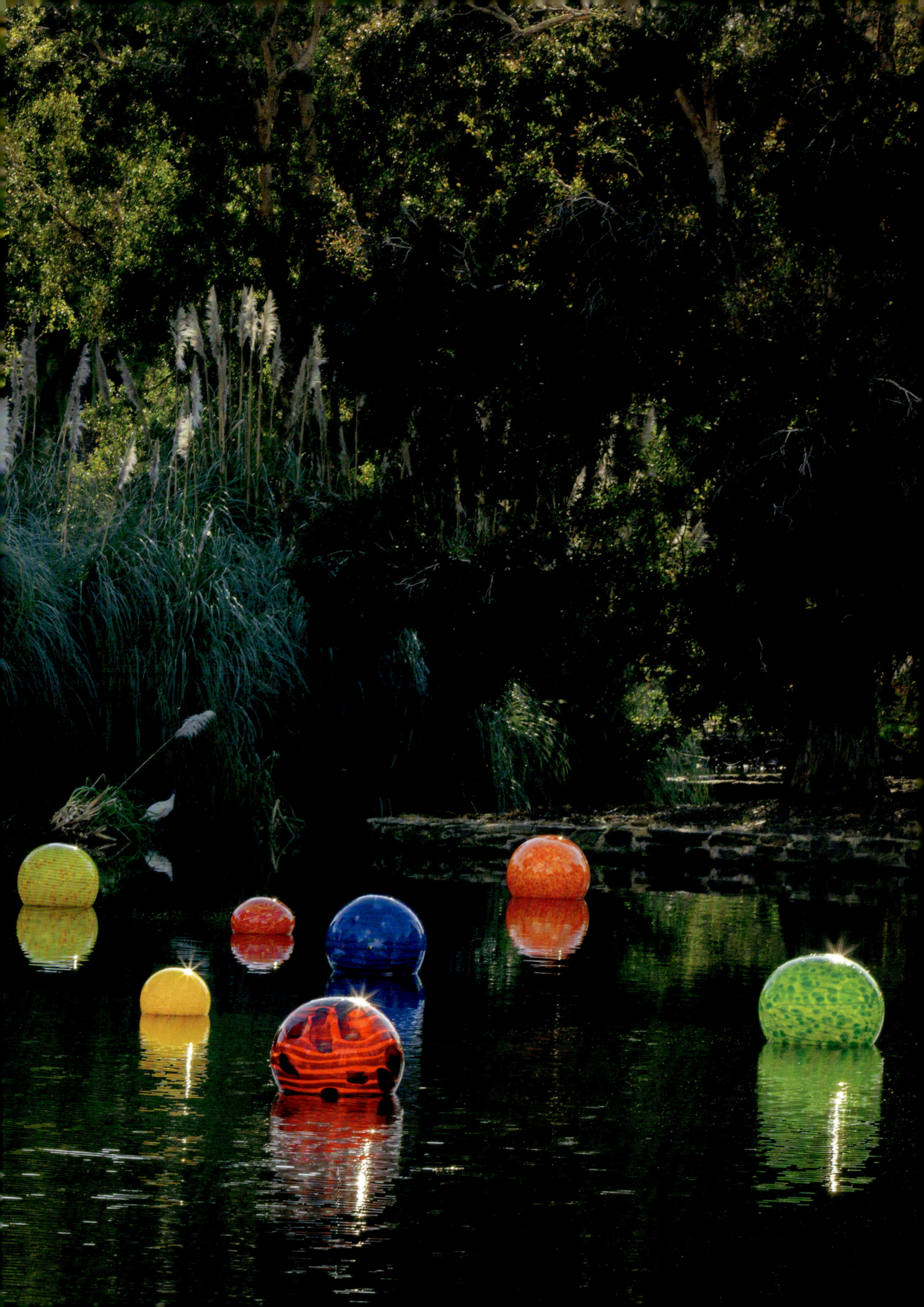

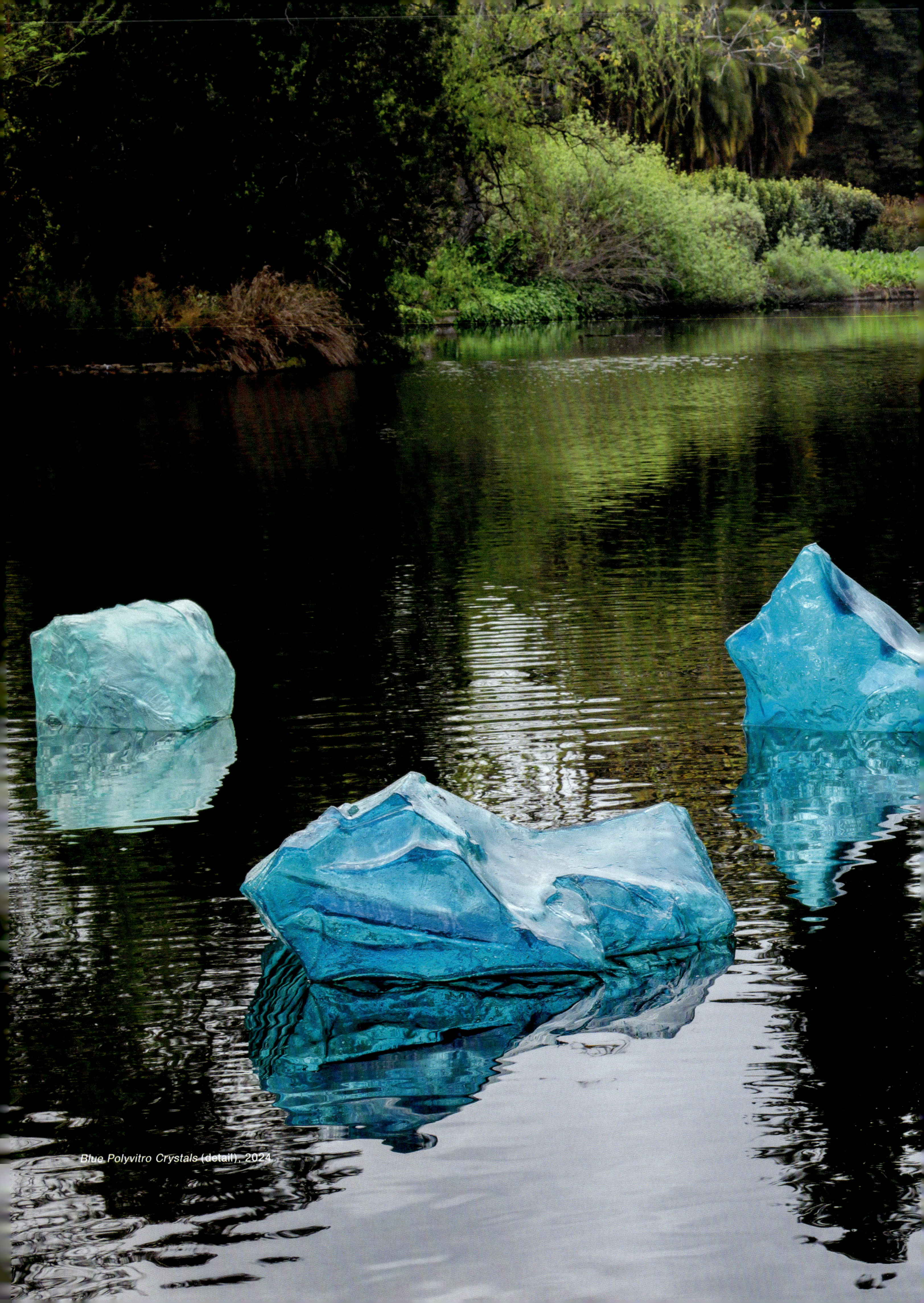

Blue Polyvitro Crystals (detail), 2024

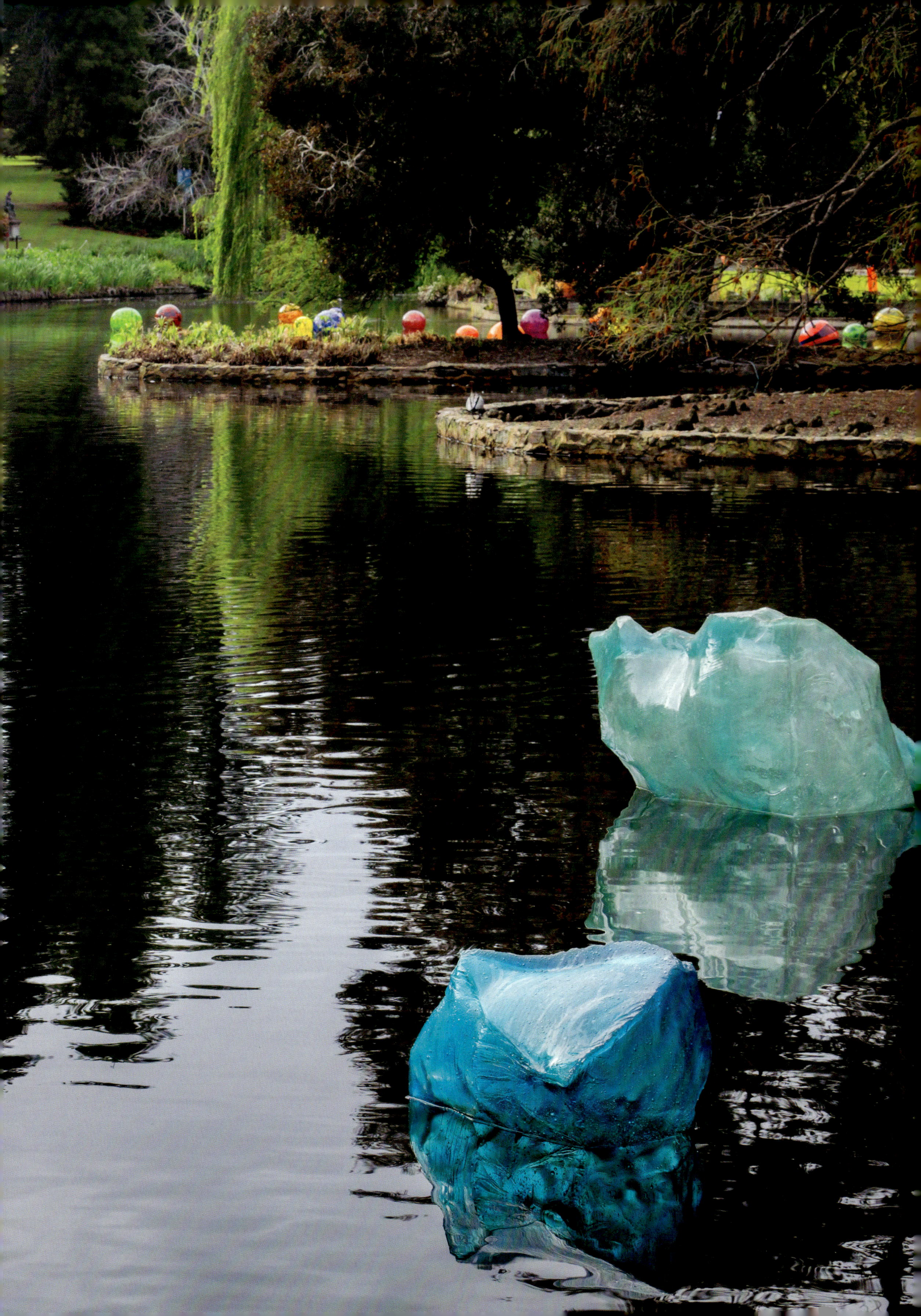

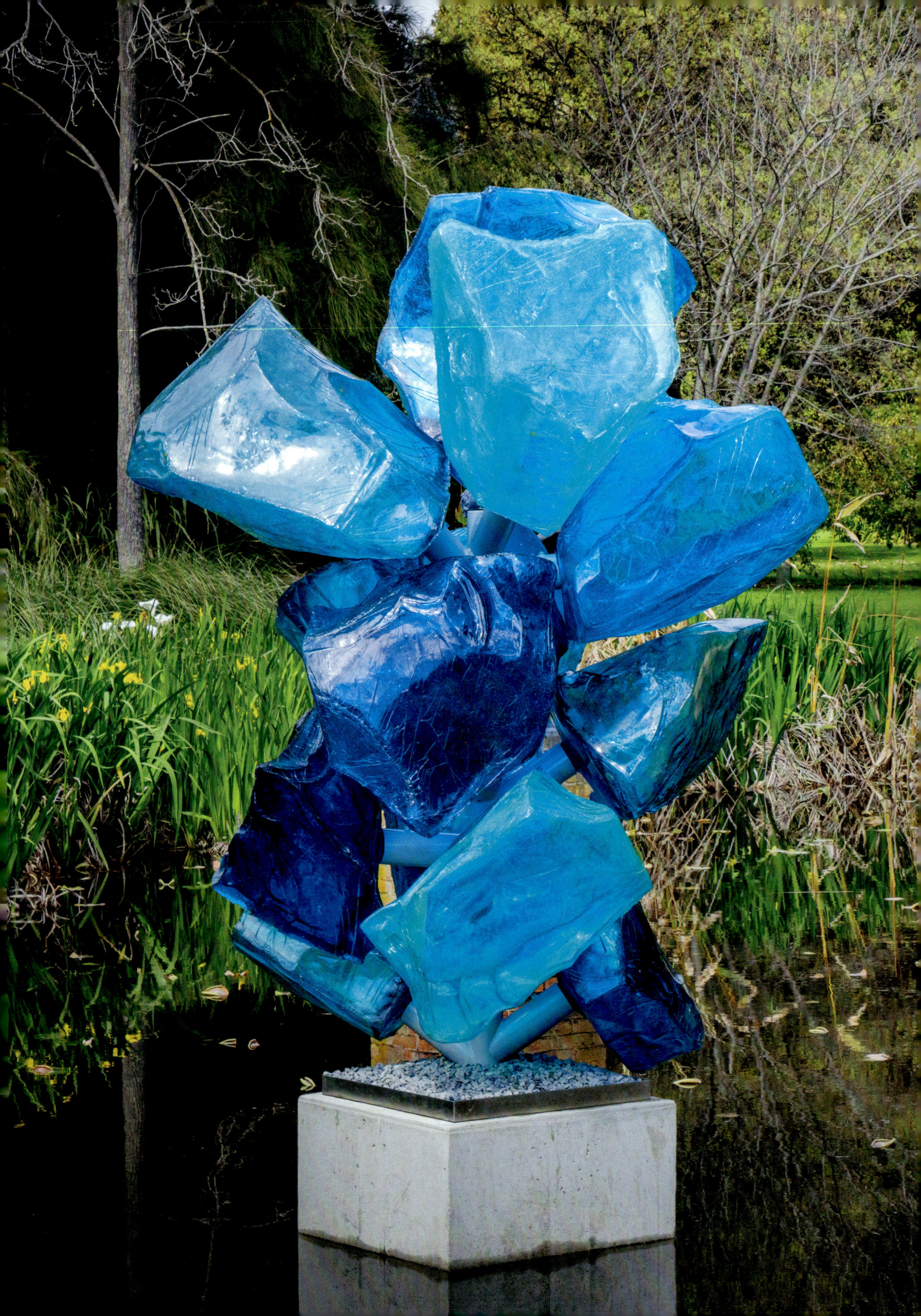

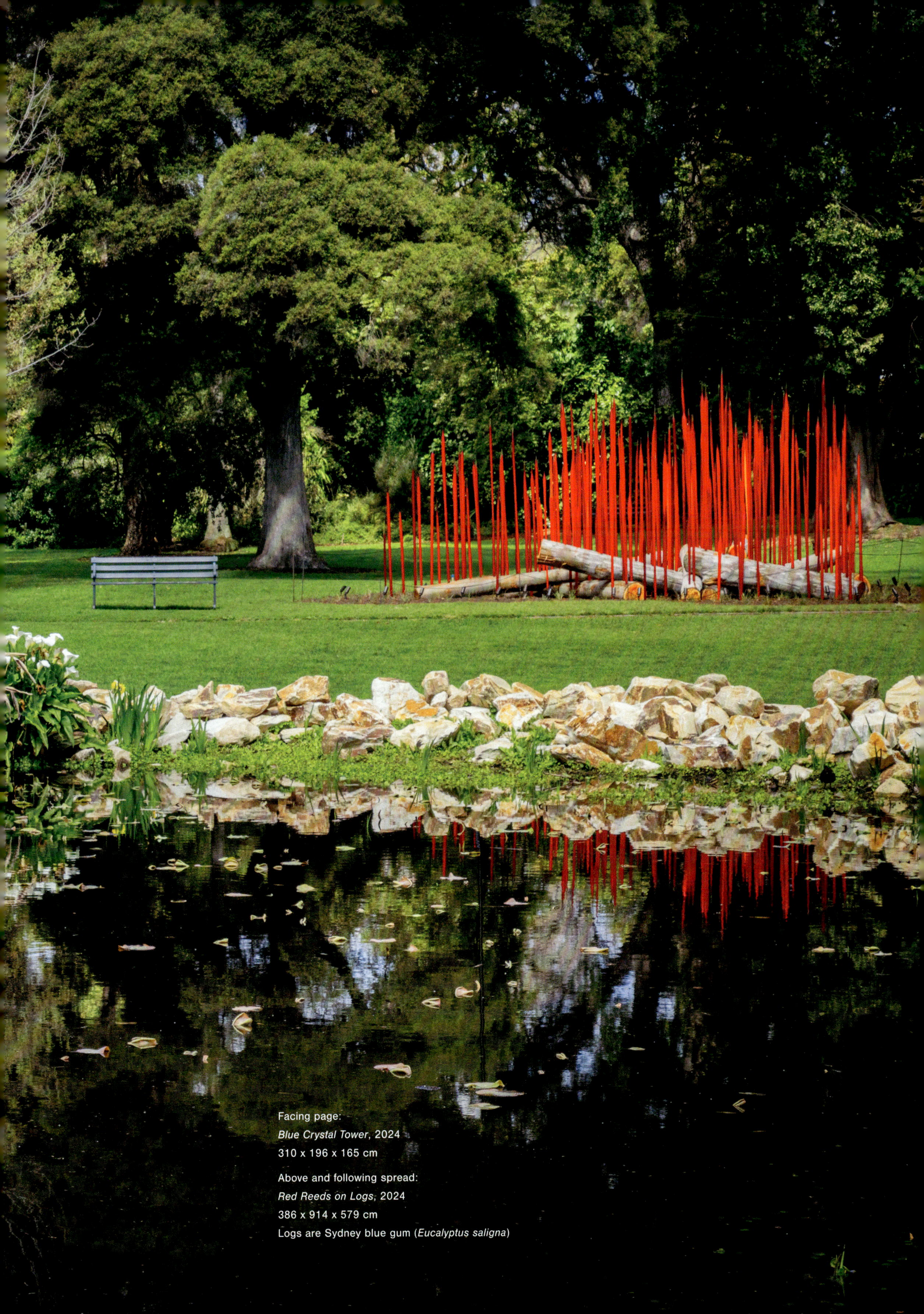

Facing page:
Blue Crystal Tower, 2024
310 x 196 x 165 cm

Above and following spread:
Red Reeds on Logs, 2024
386 x 914 x 579 cm
Logs are Sydney blue gum (*Eucalyptus saligna*)

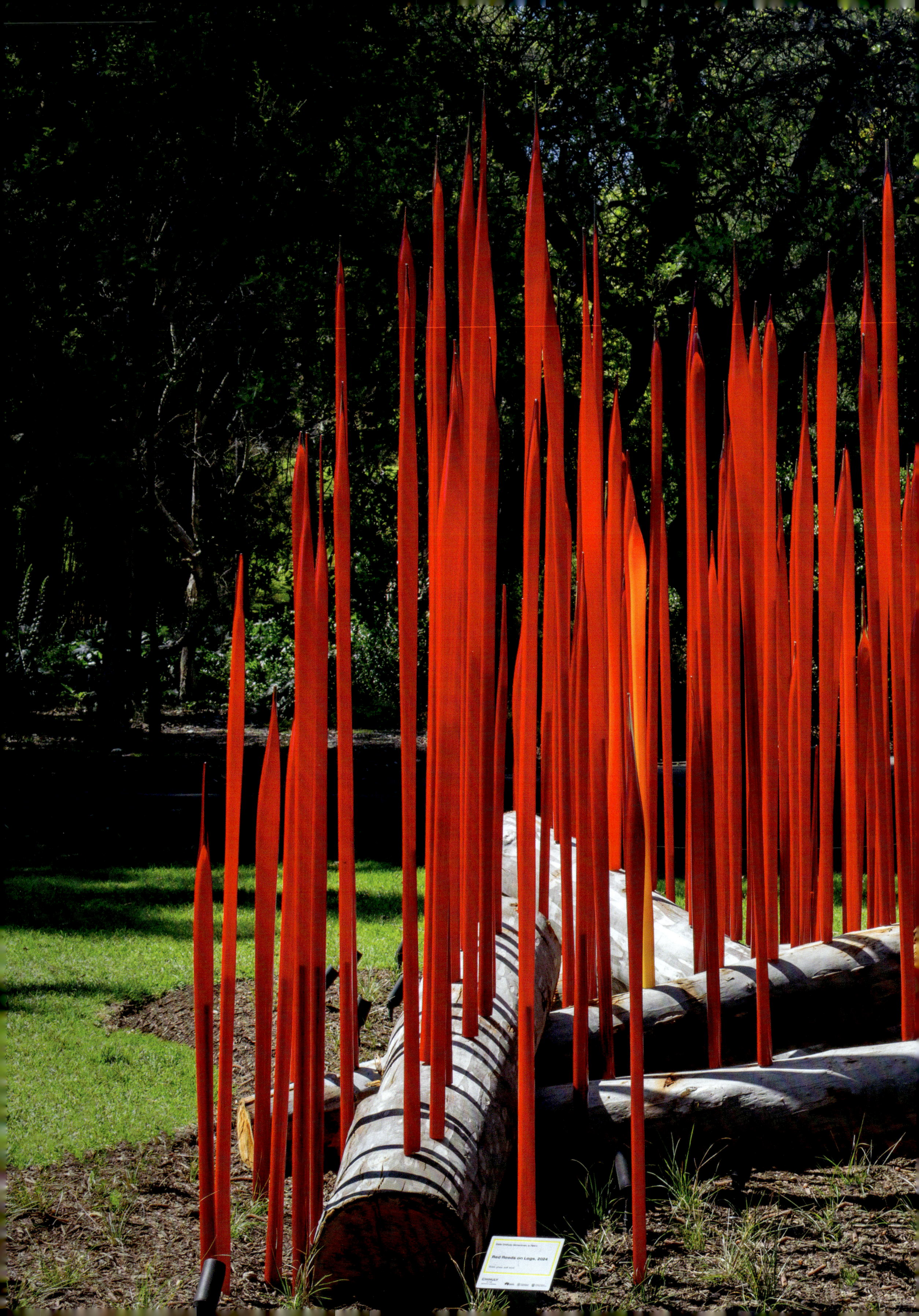
Red Reeds on Logs, 2024
CHIHULY

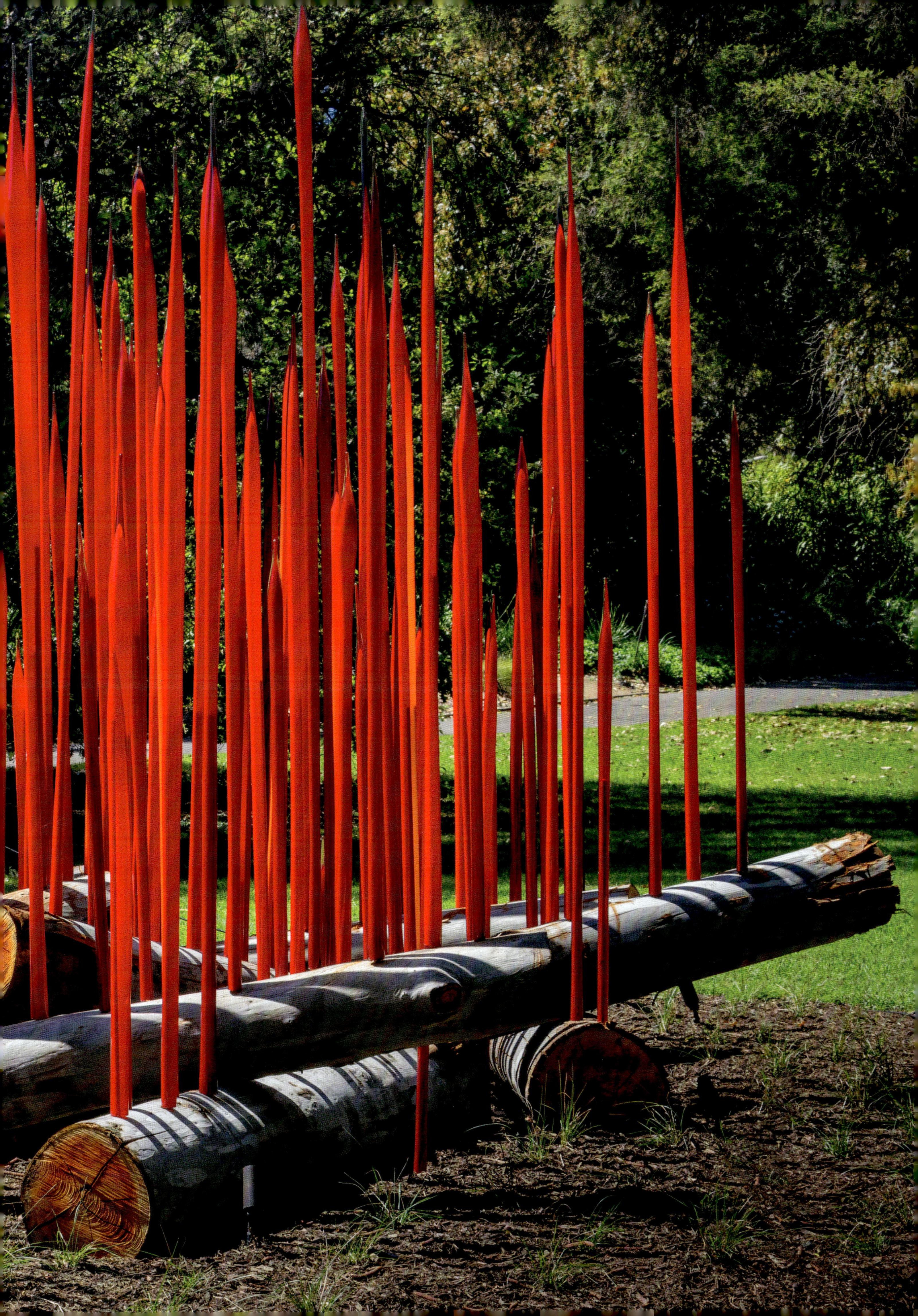

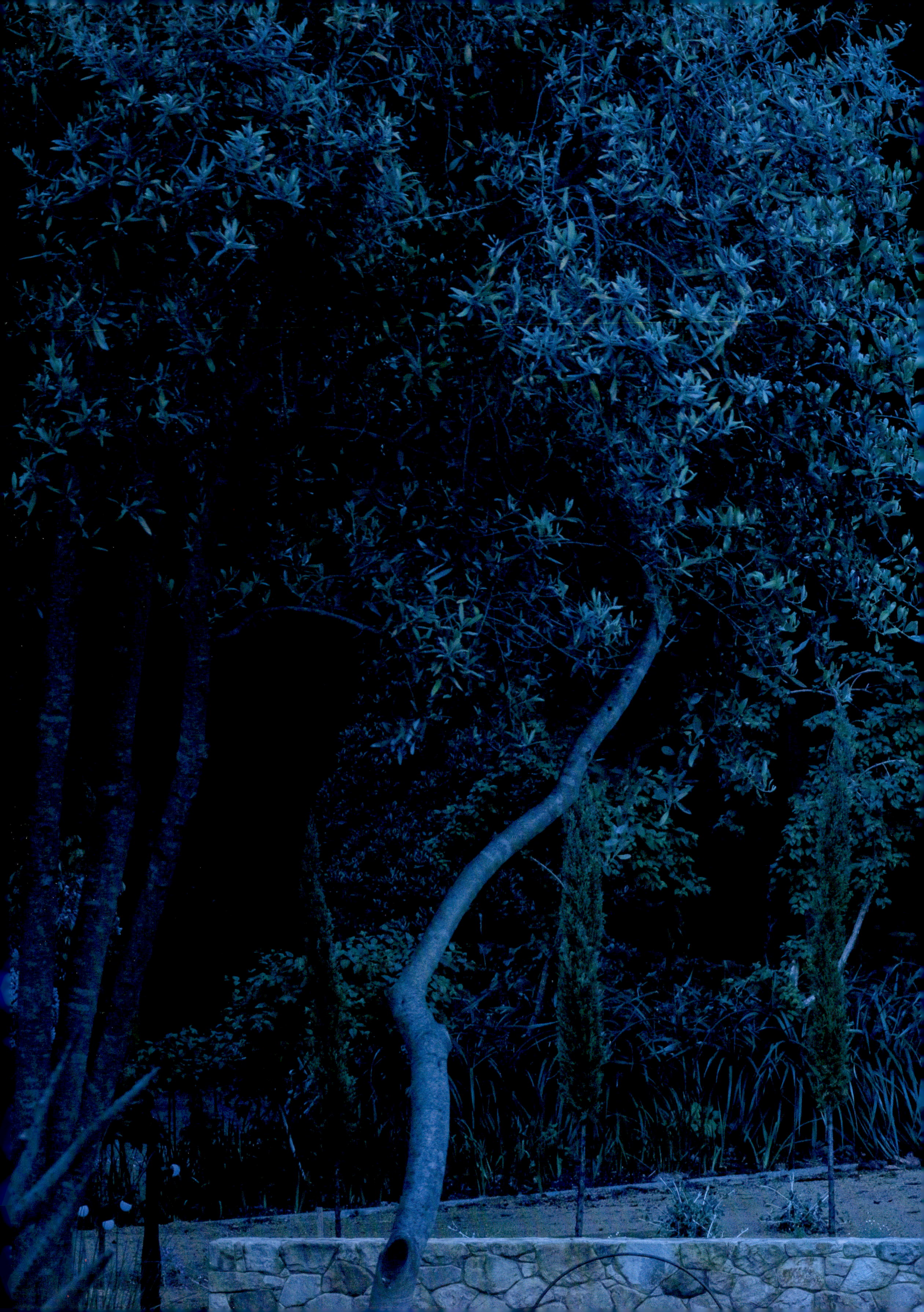

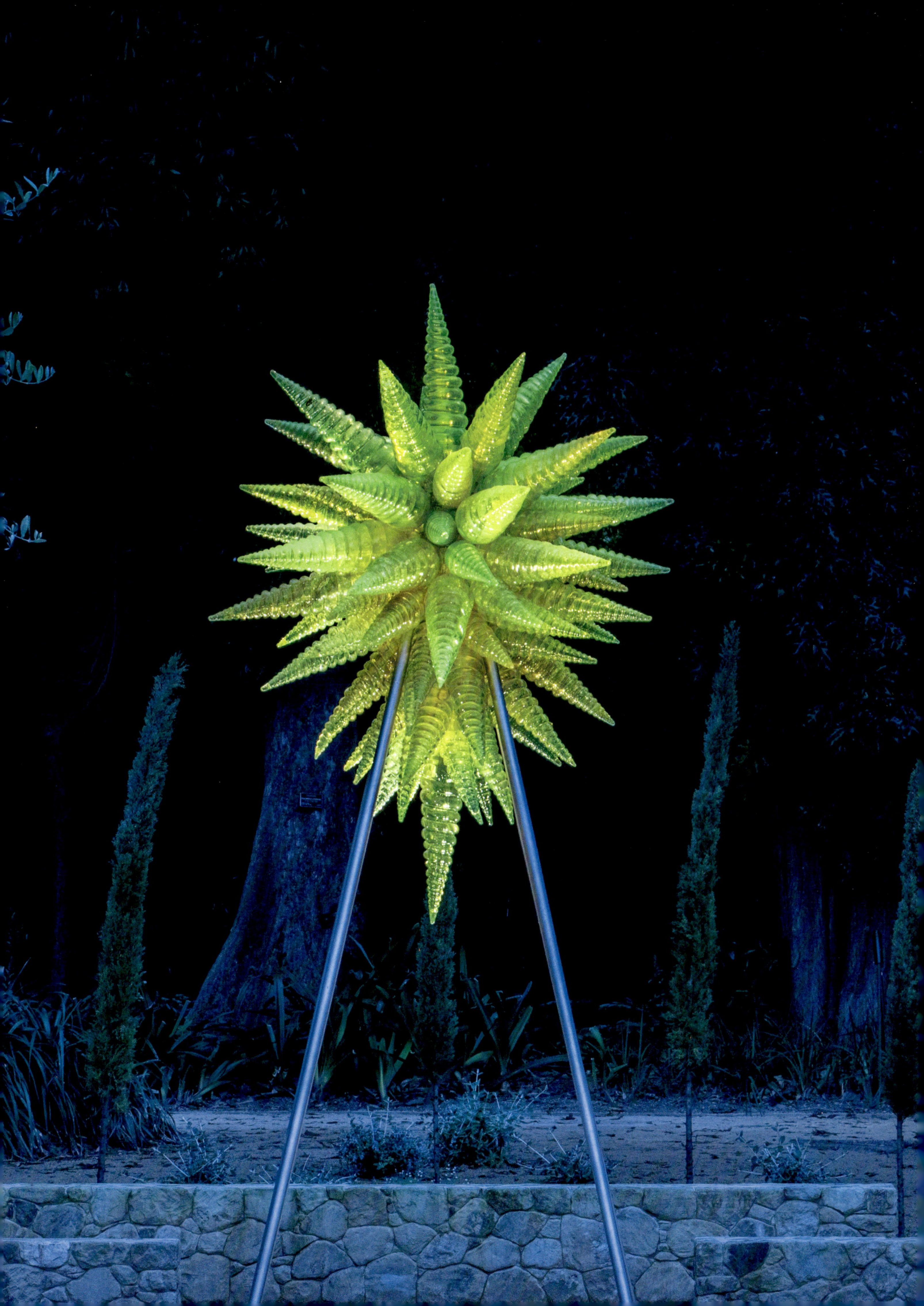

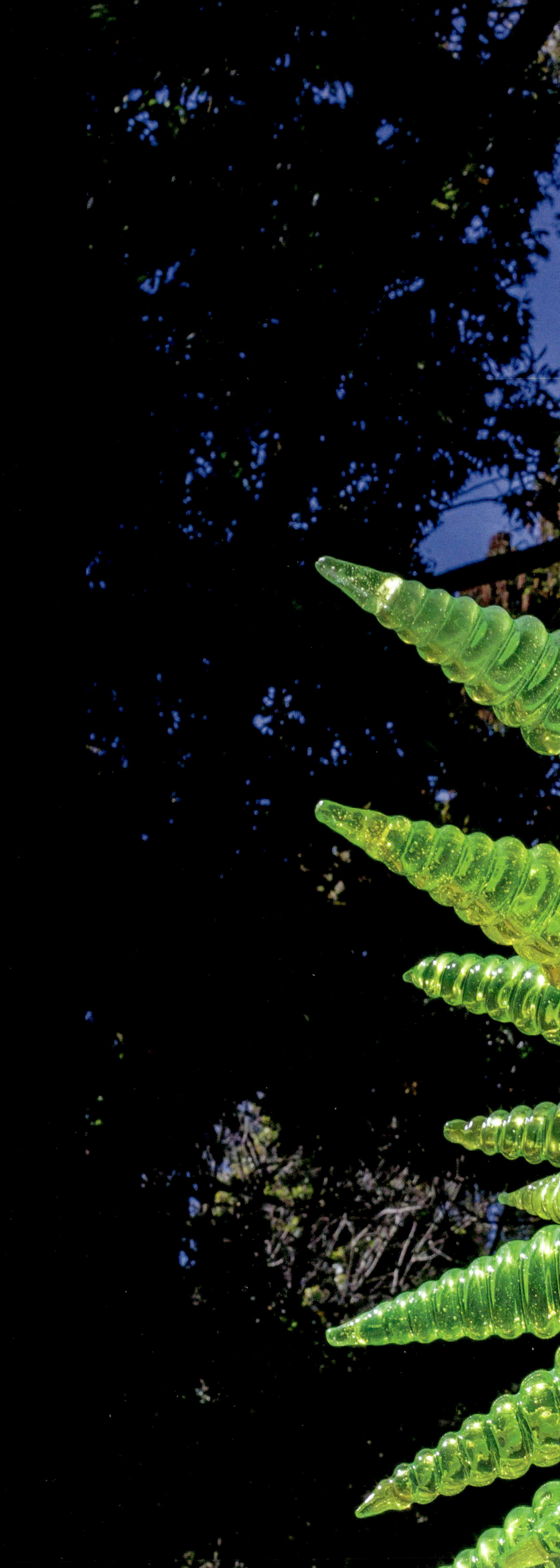

Previous and this spread:
Chartreuse Hornet Polyvitro Chandelier, 2001
241 x 180 x 165 cm

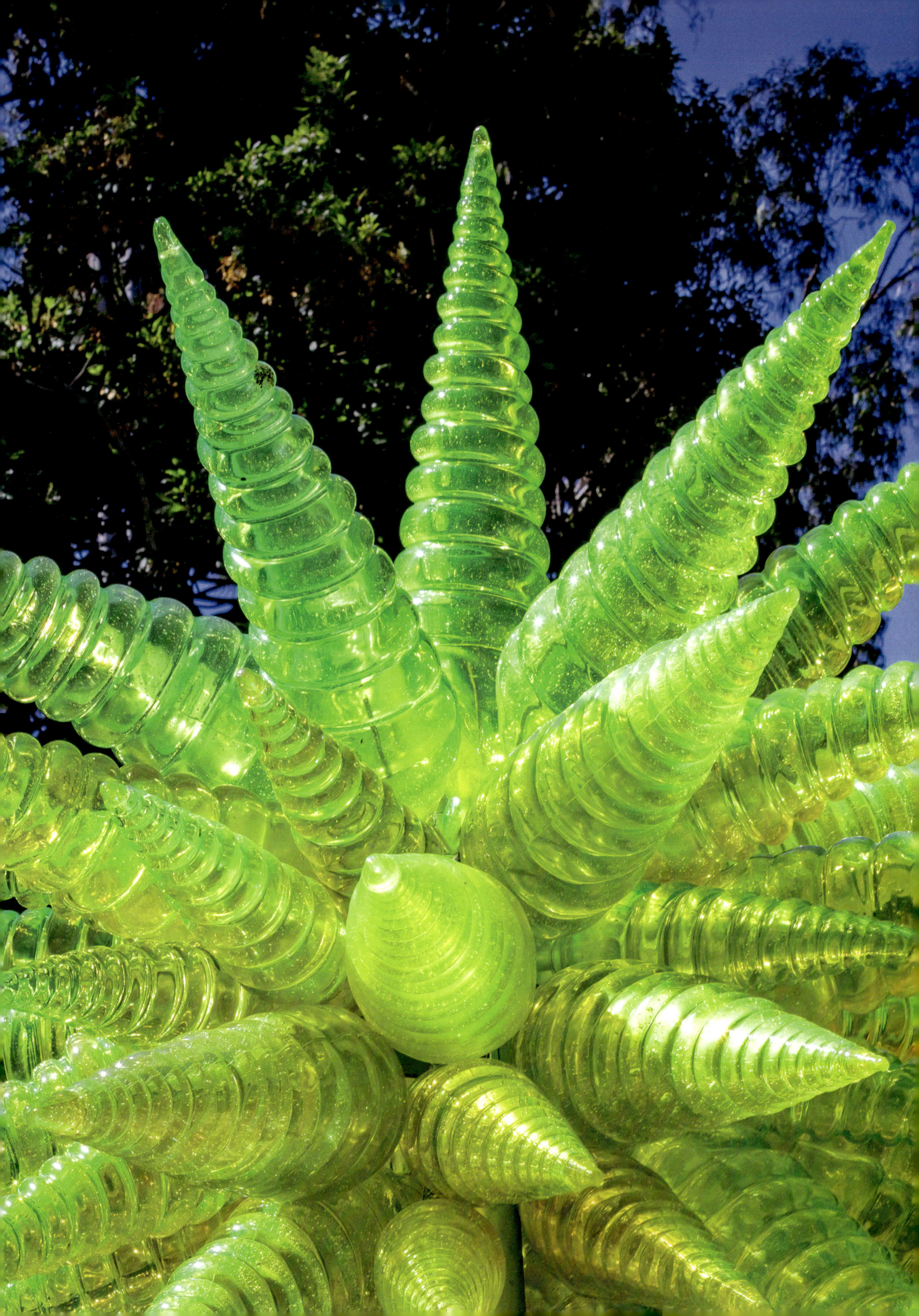

Vivid Lime Icicle Tower, 2022

622 x 244 x 244 cm

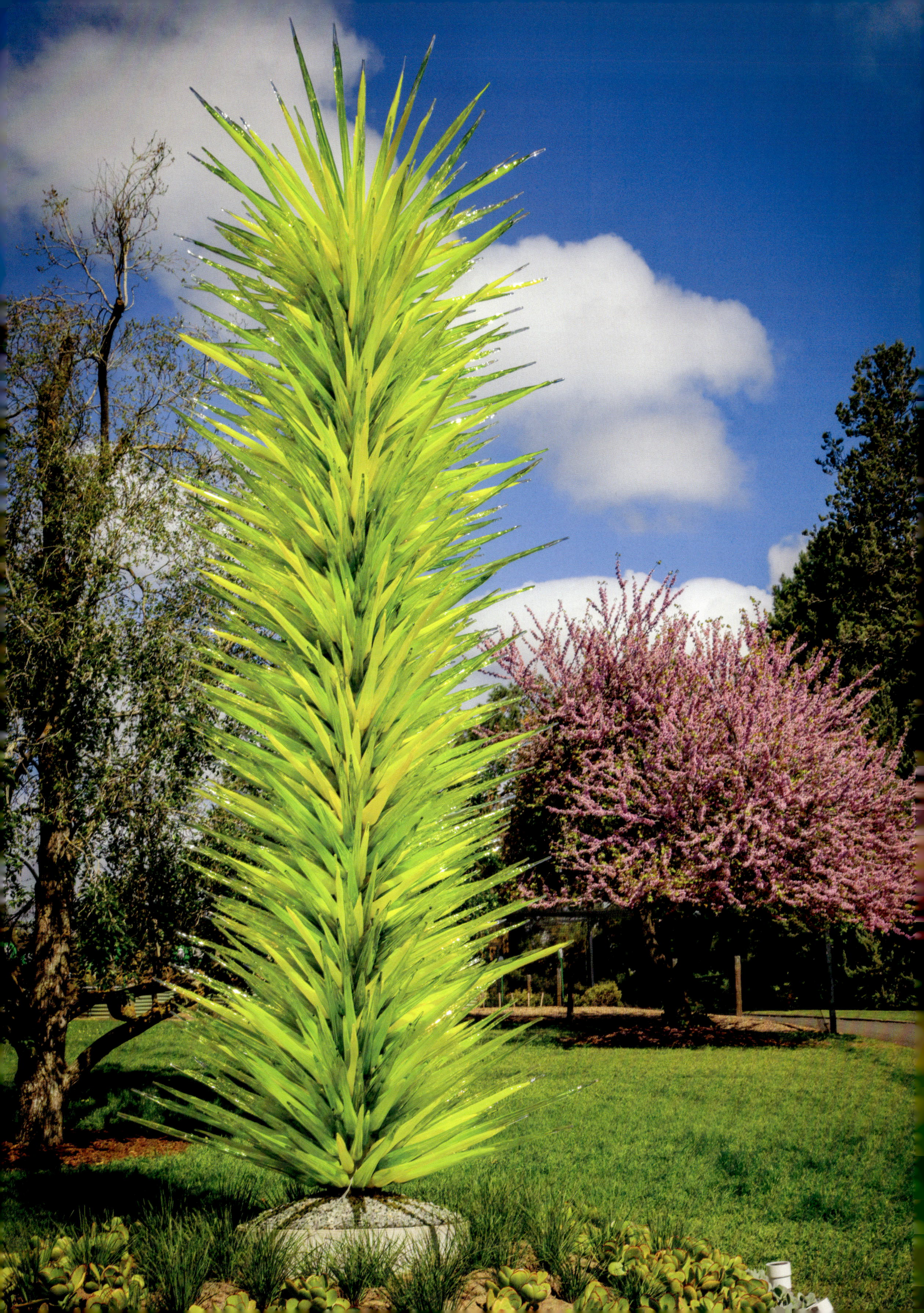

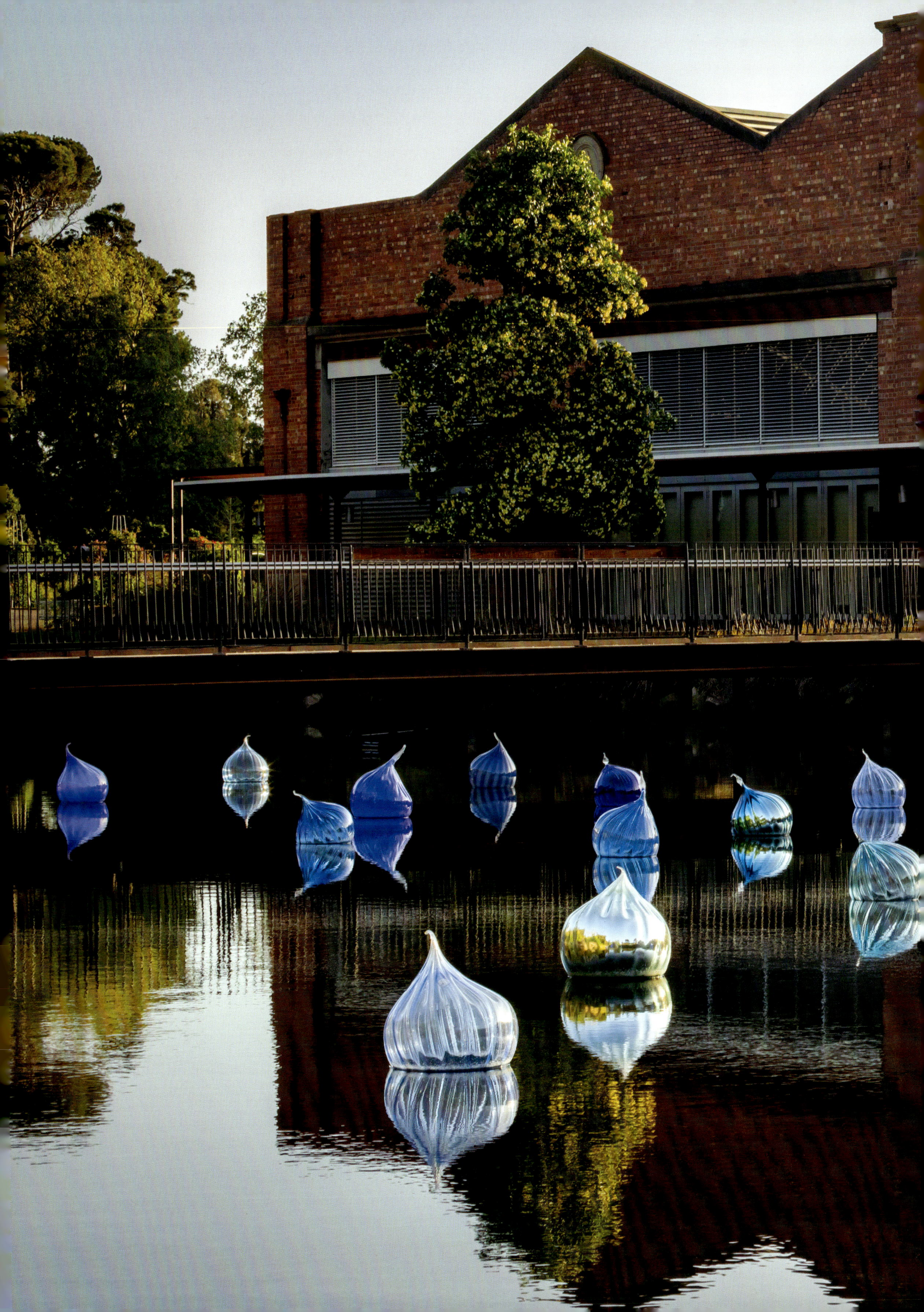

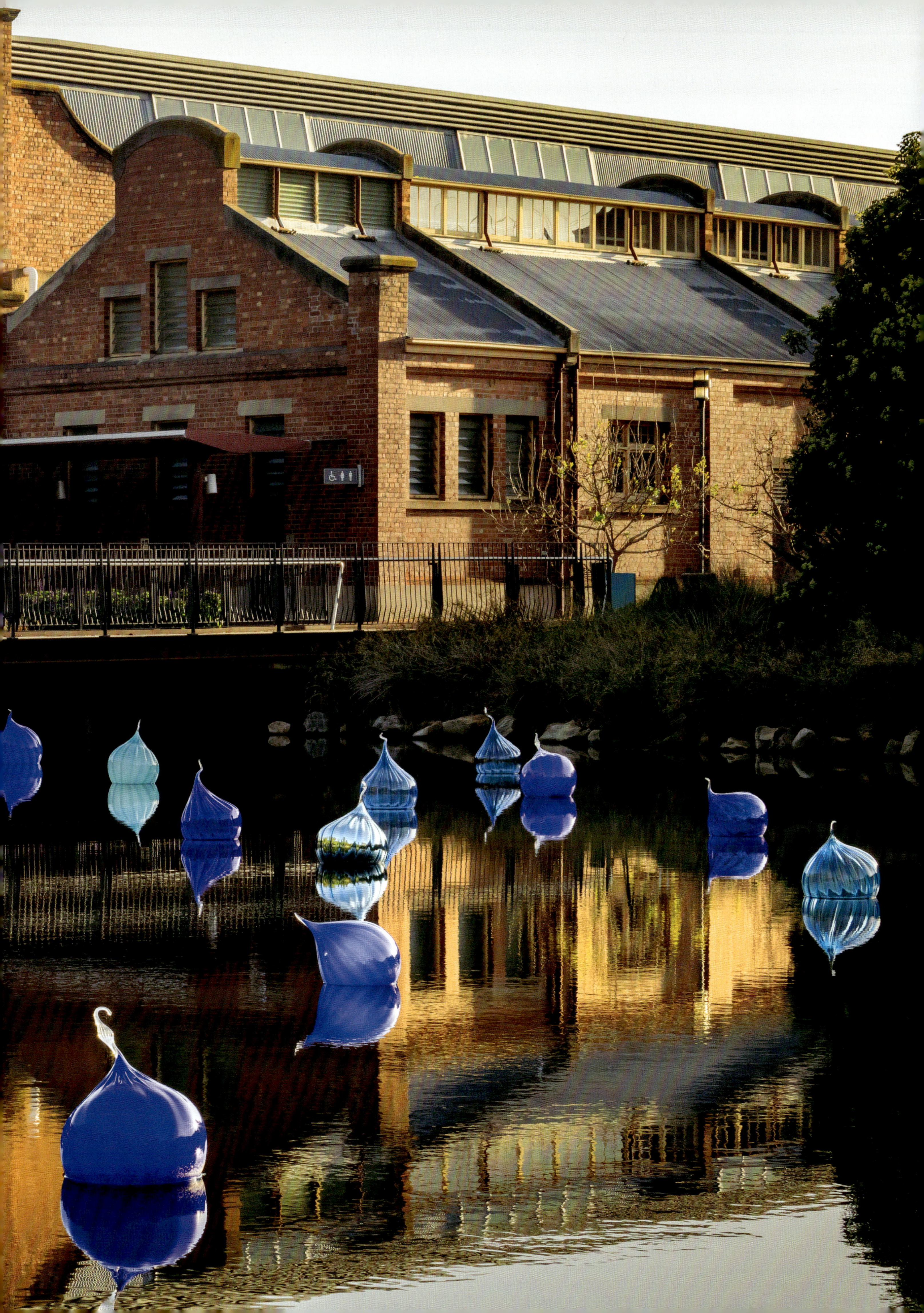

Previous spread and facing page:
Walla Wallas, 2024

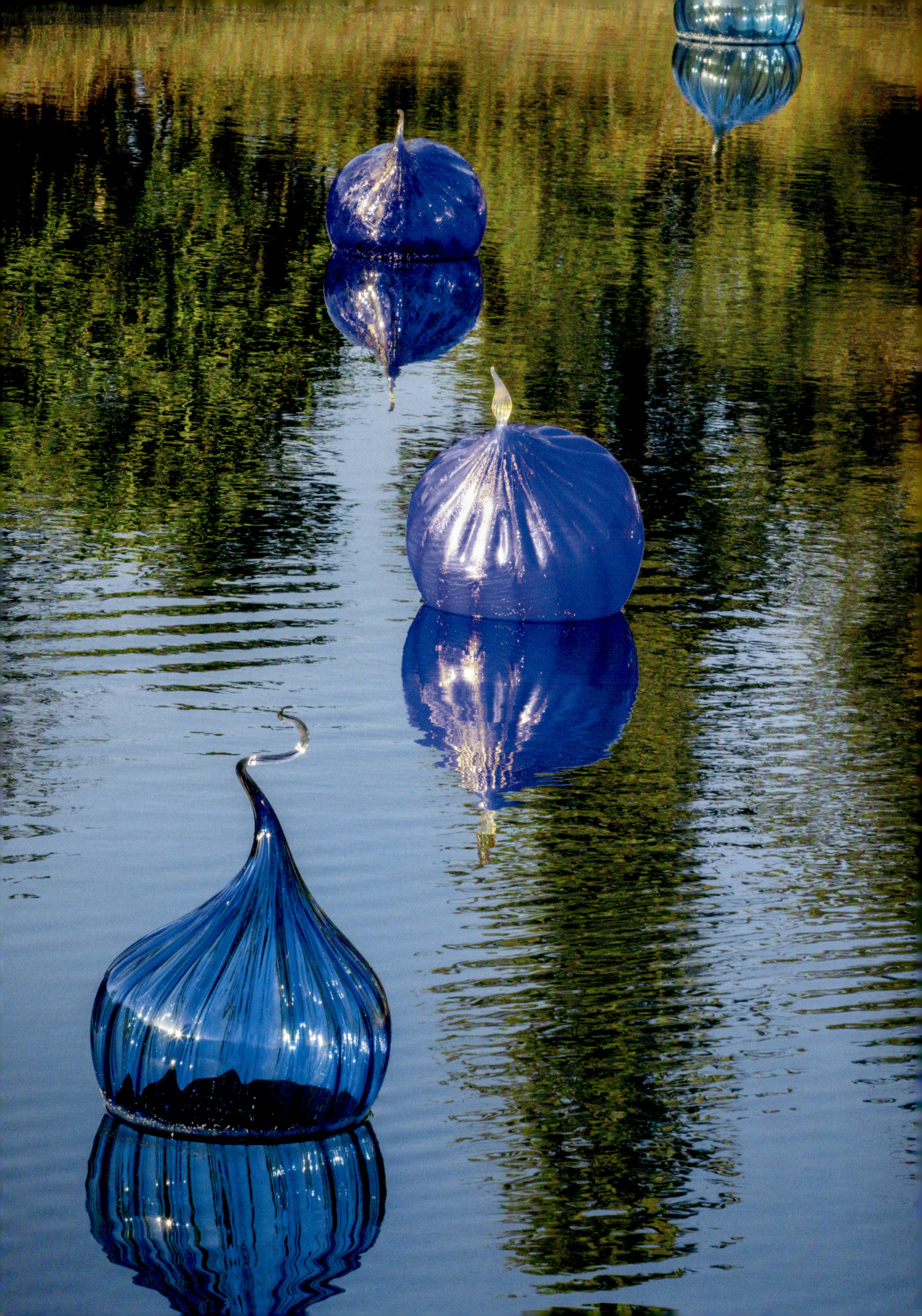

This spread and following:

Lime and Lava Red Tower, 2021

472 x 224 x 224 cm

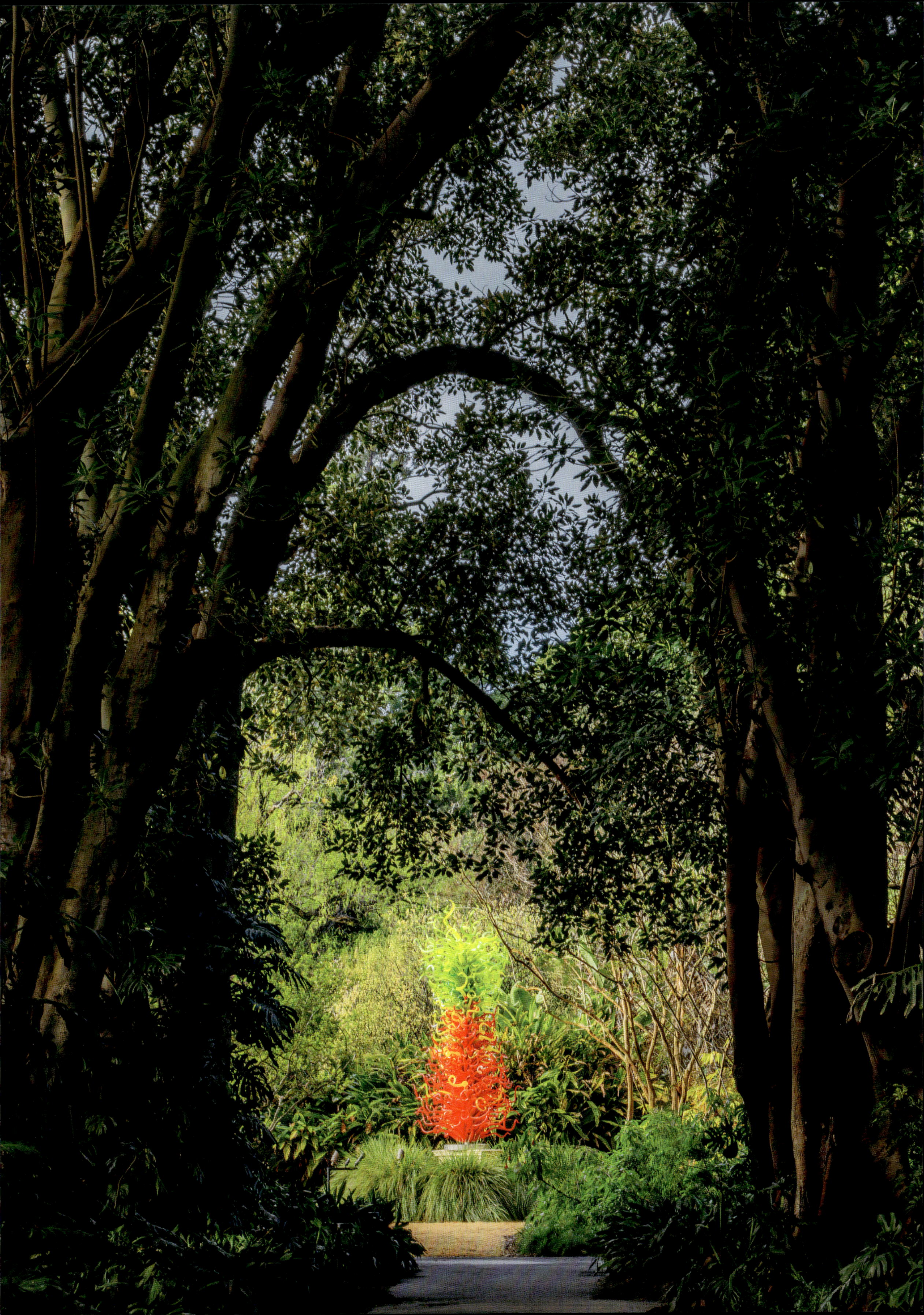

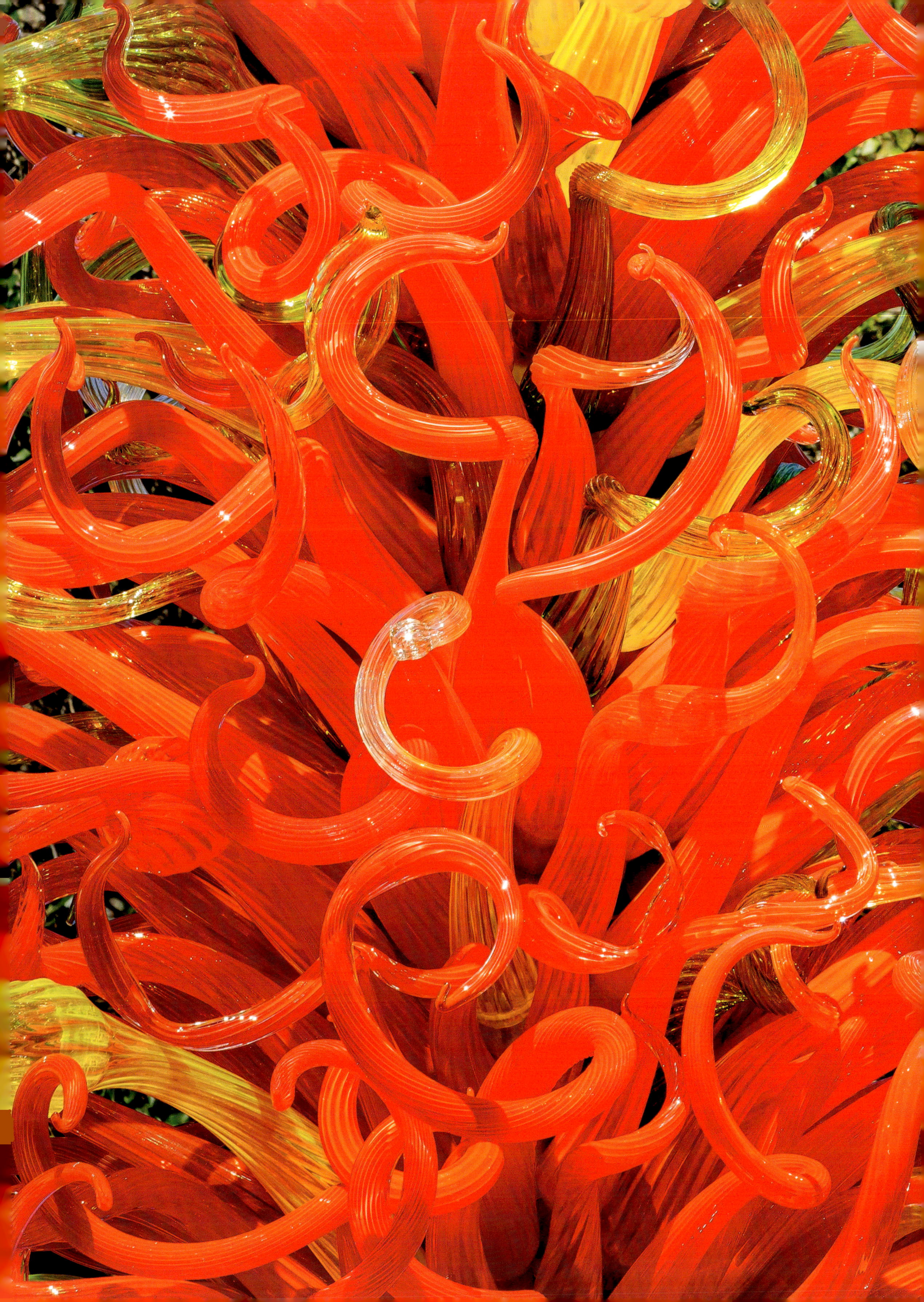

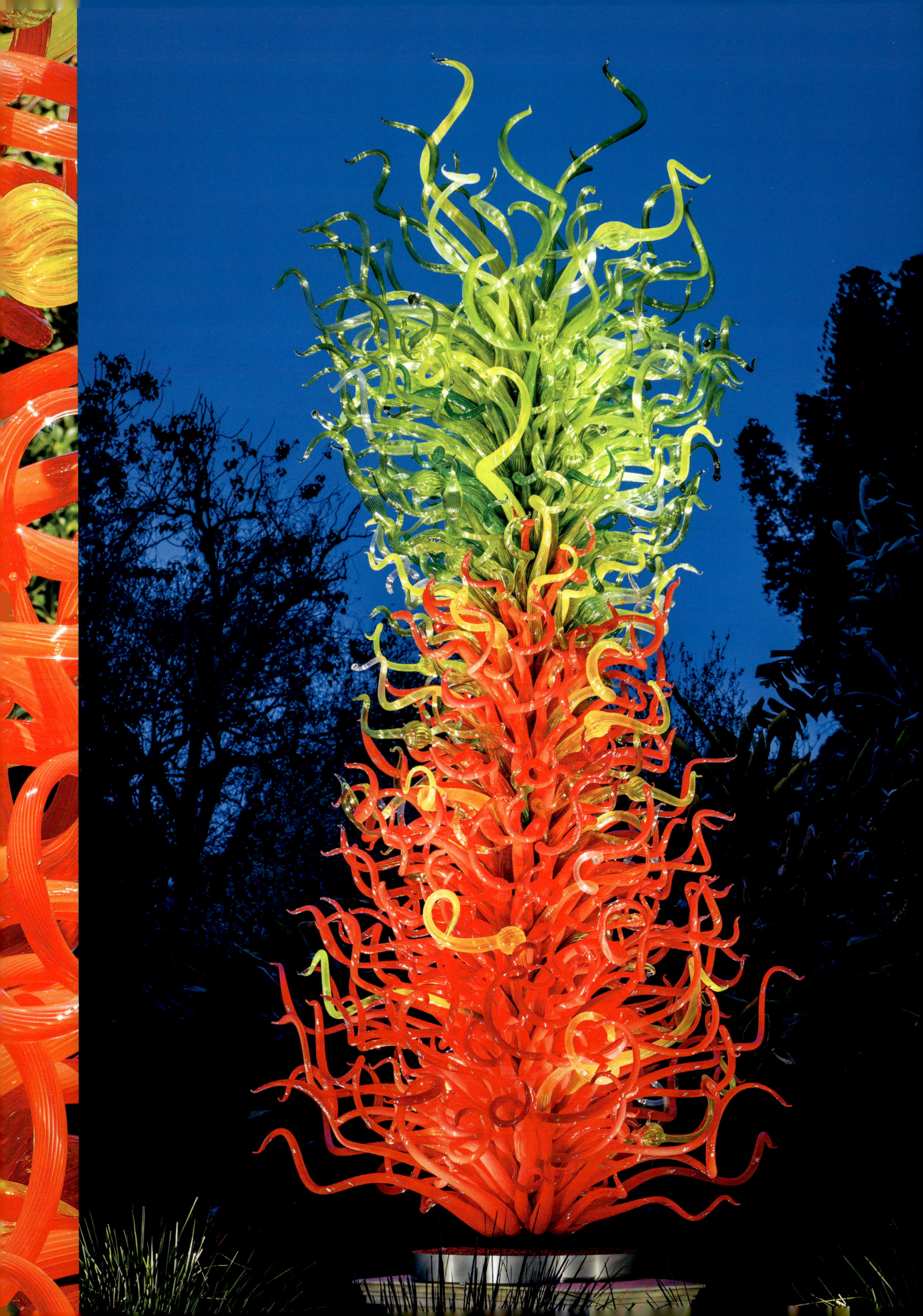

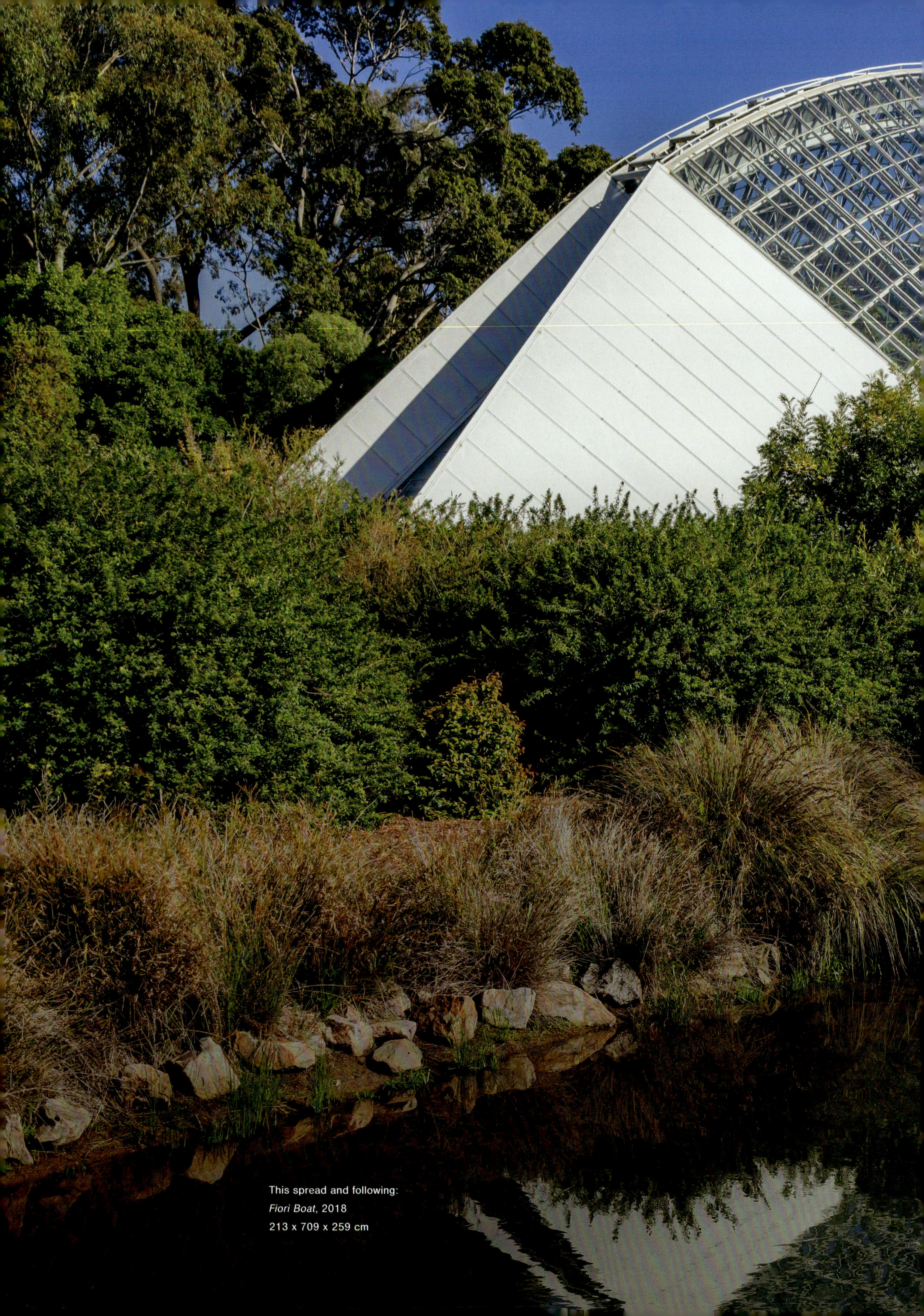

This spread and following:
Fiori Boat, 2018
213 x 709 x 259 cm

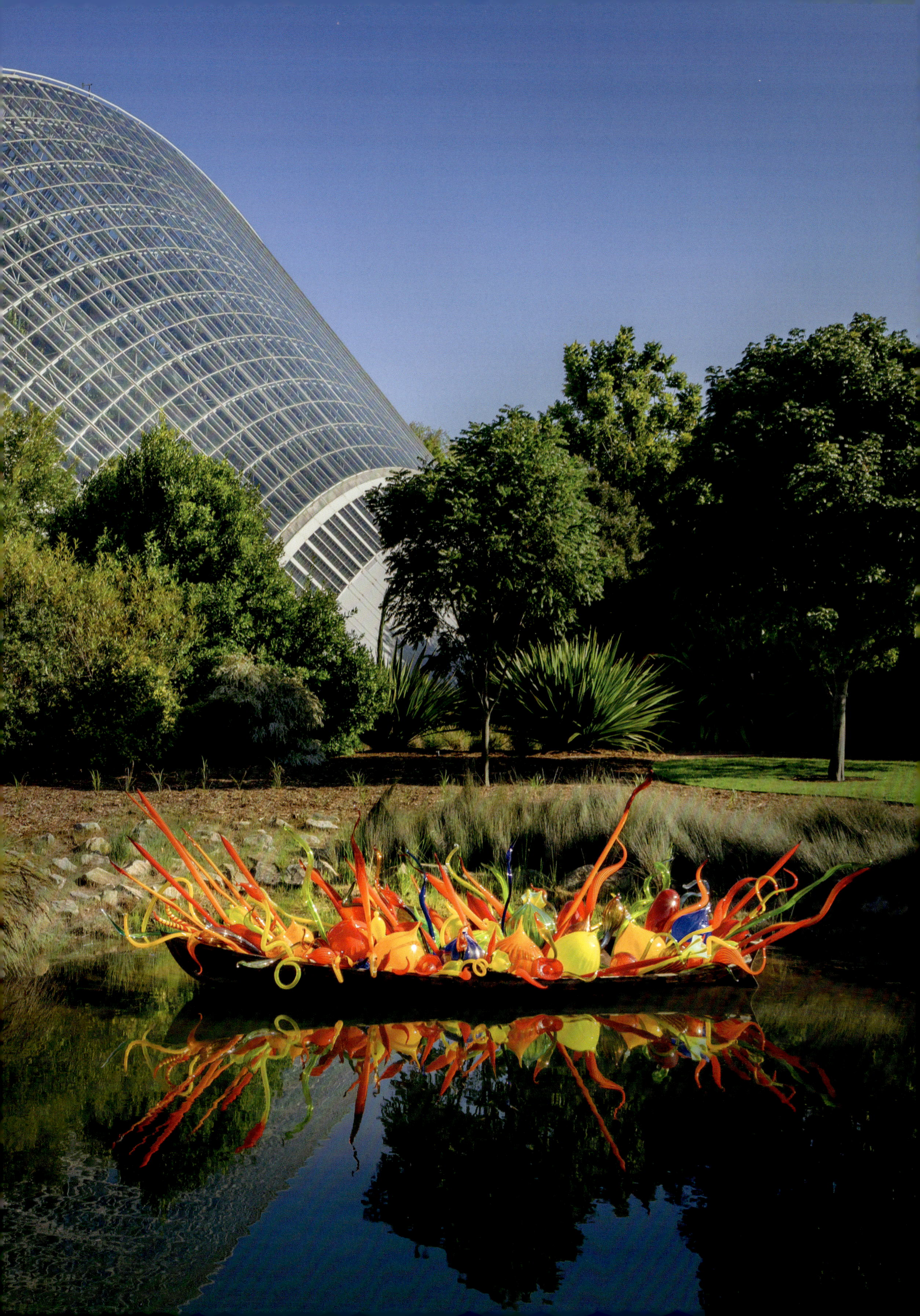

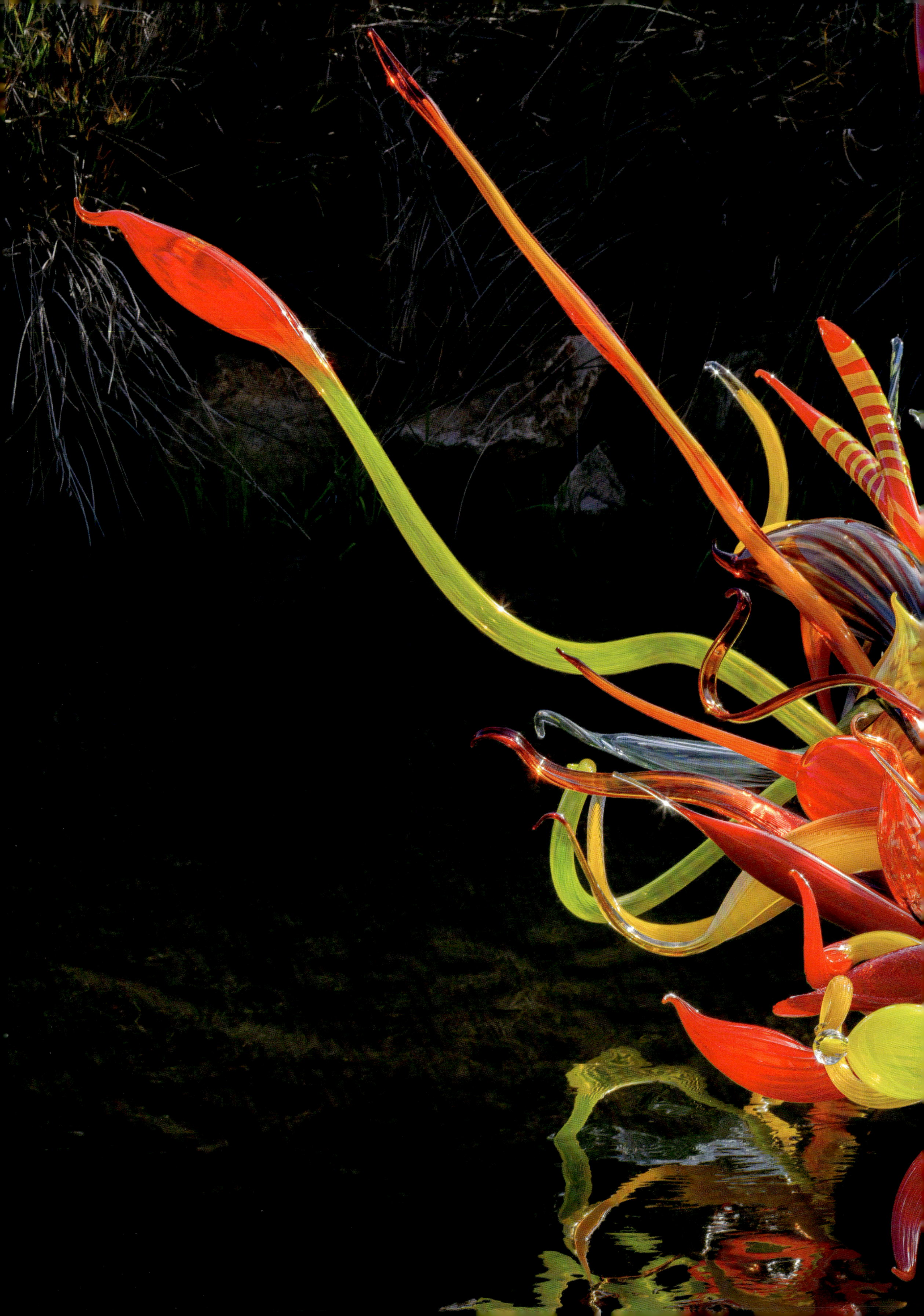

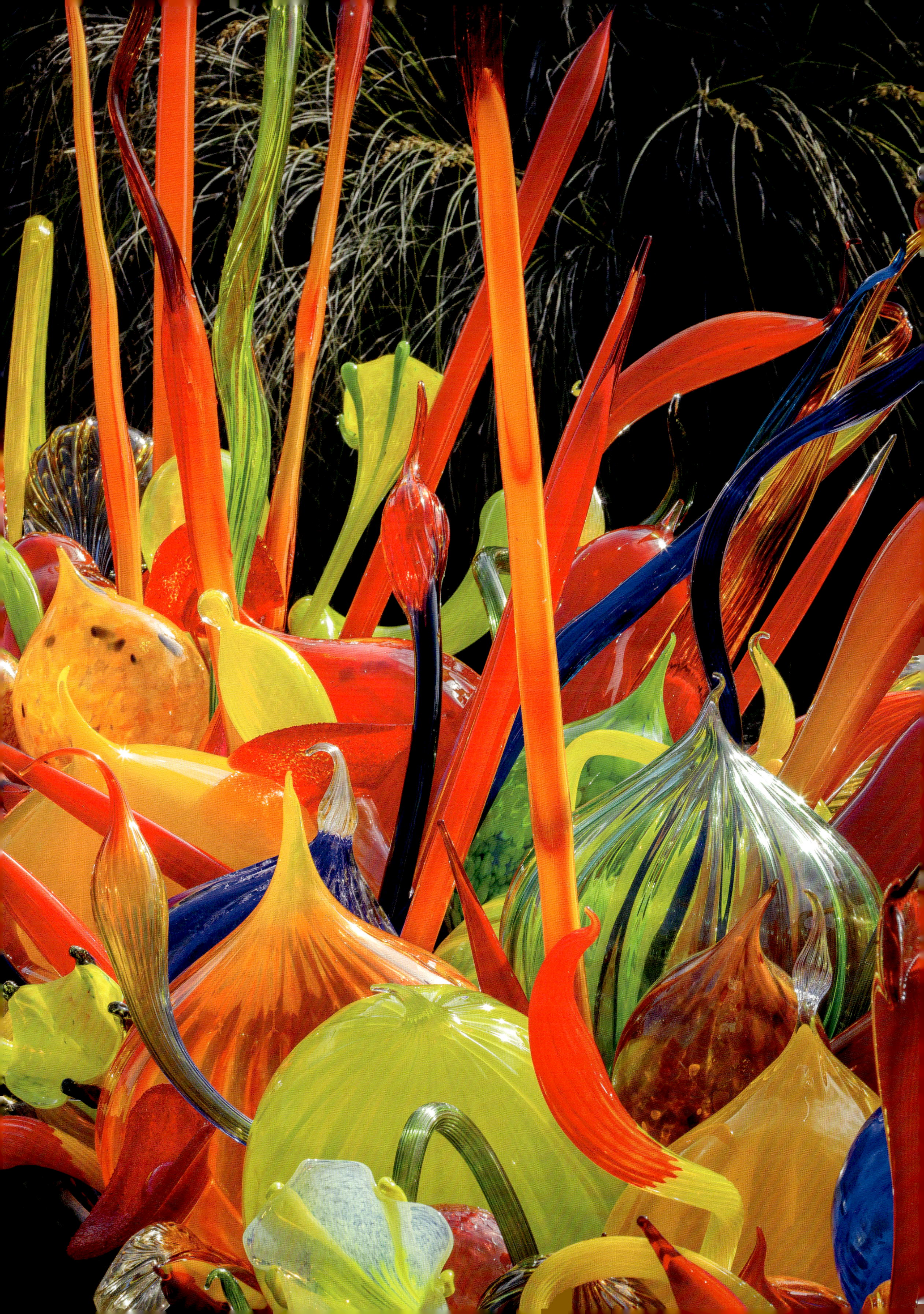

In Full Colour: Dale Chihuly

Nine groupings of exquisite smaller-scale Chihuly works emerge from the temperate rainforest of the Bicentennial Conservatory, enhanced by a unique exhibition that offers a deep dive into the world of this maverick in molten glass—his career milestones, his inspirations. his revolutionary techniques, his installations outdoors and his impact on the vibrant Australian glass scene.

Mottled Trumpet Flowers and Plum Feathers, 2024
201 x 183 x 137 cm

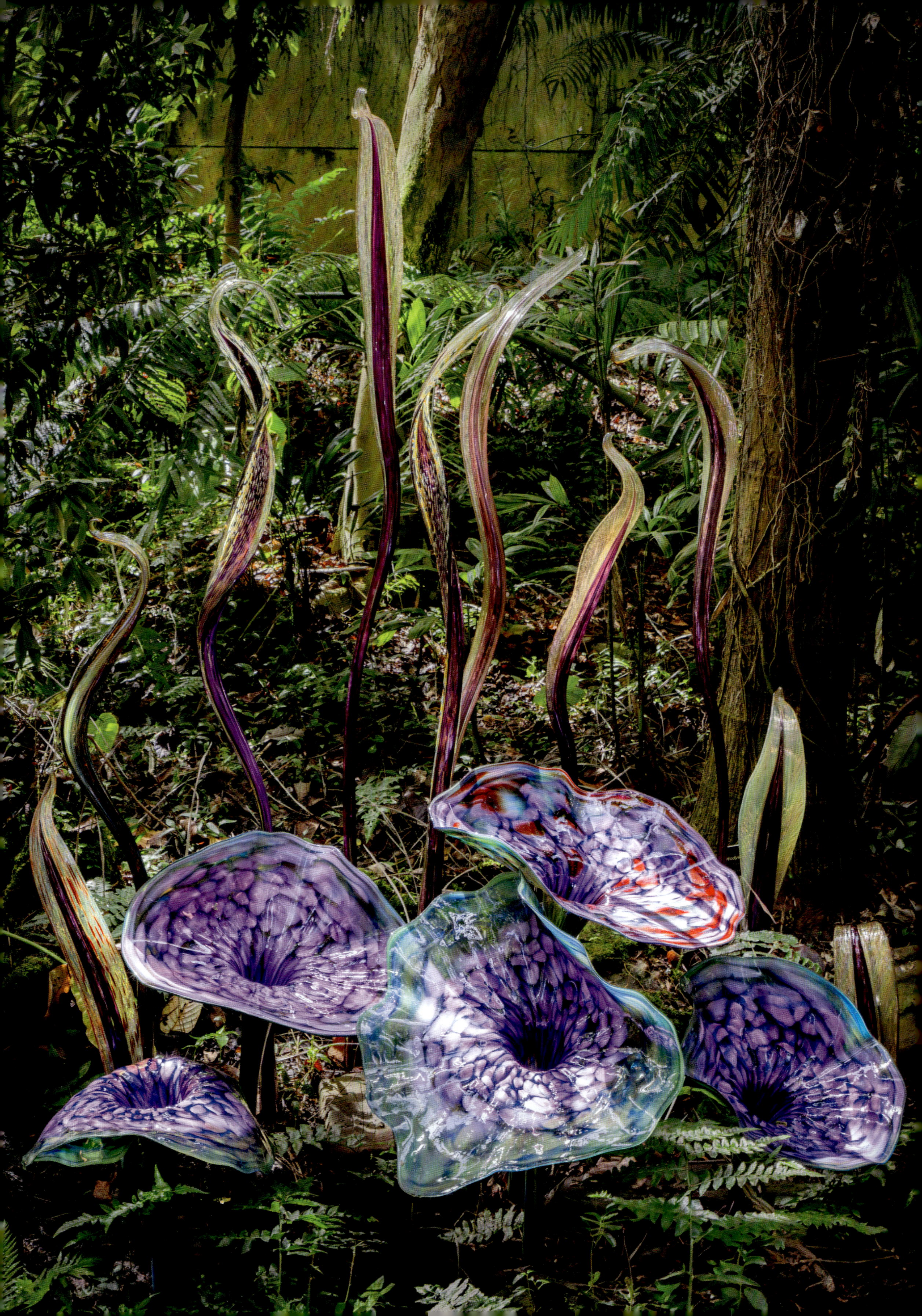

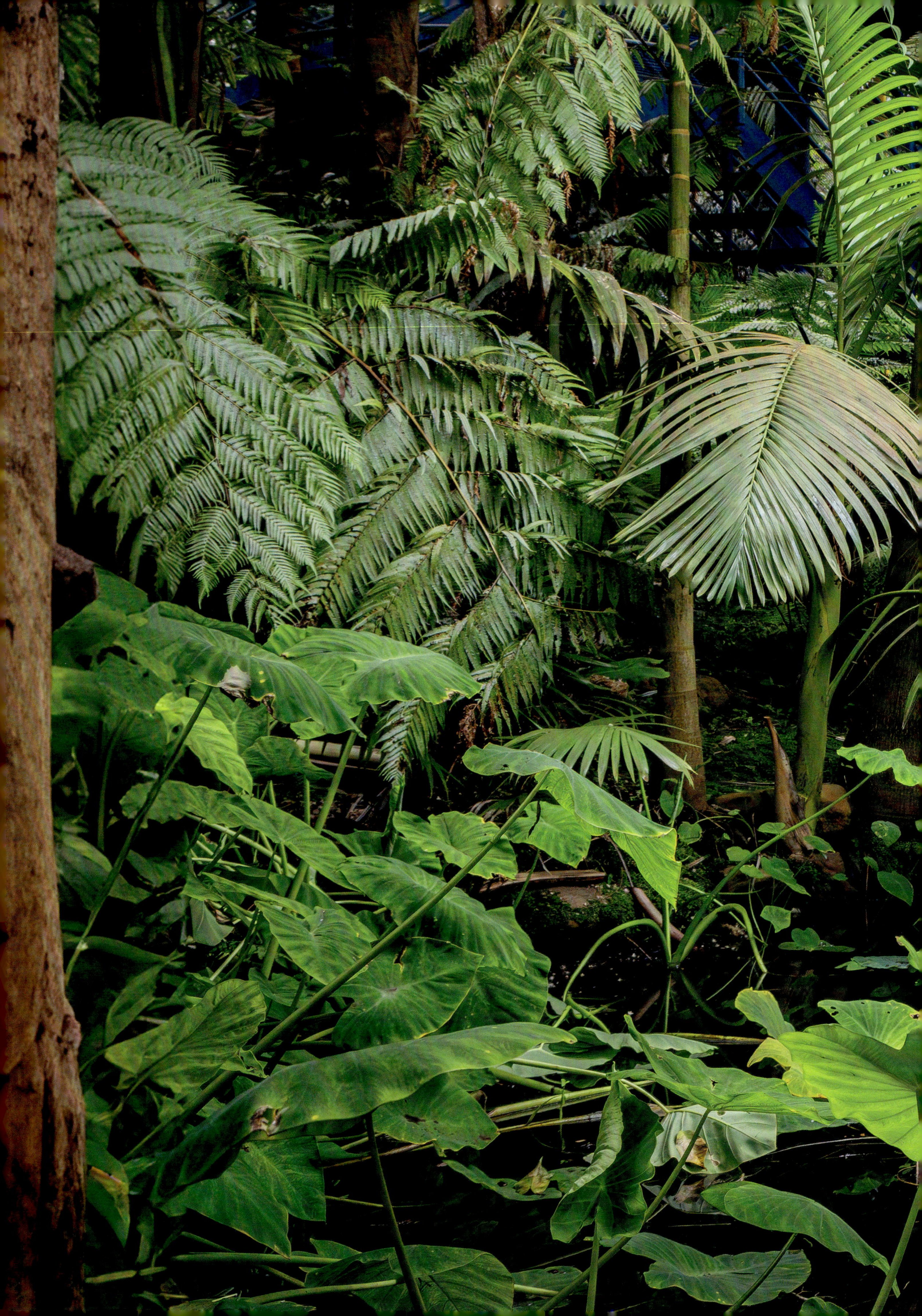

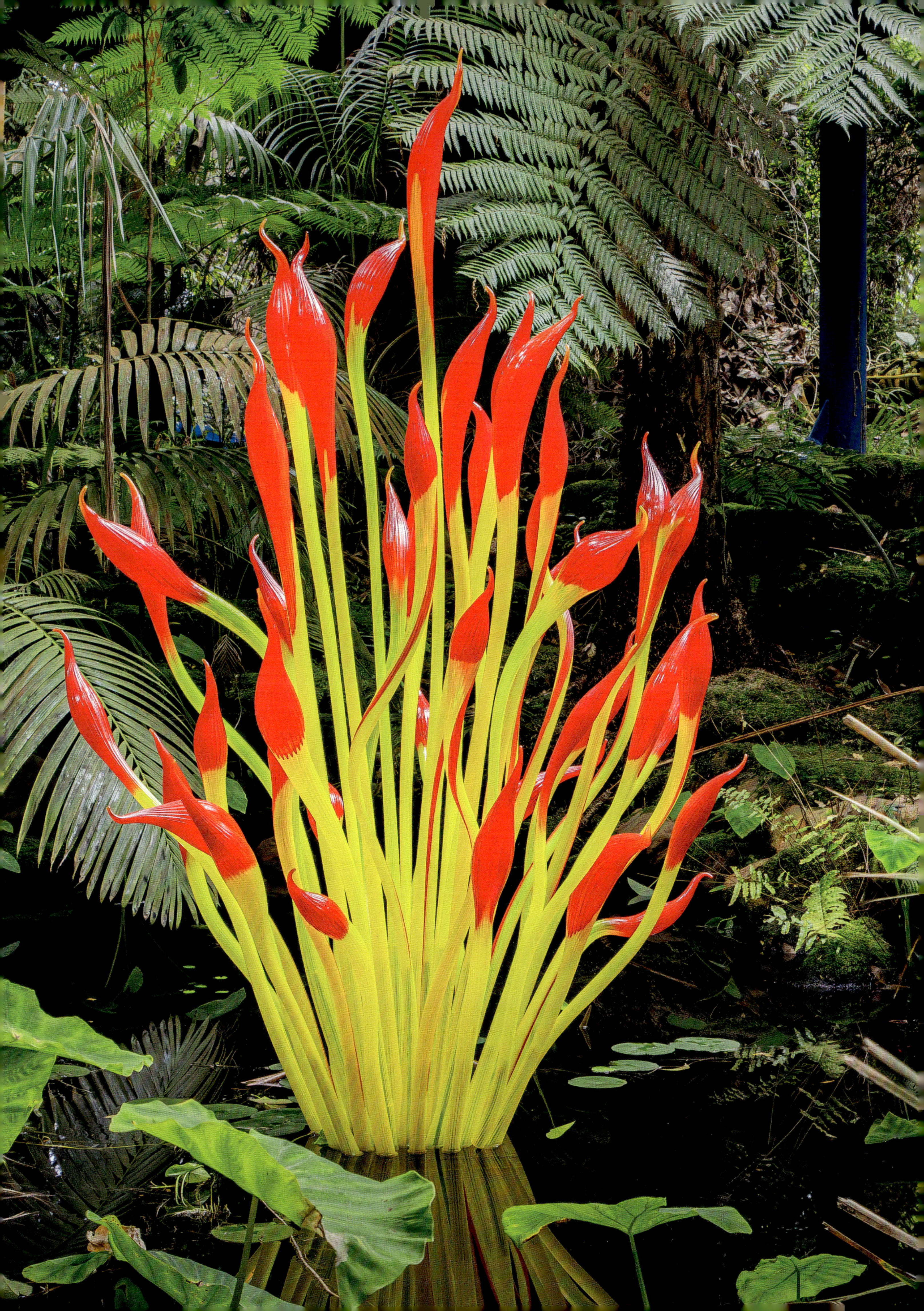

Previous spread:
Paintbrushes, 2024
224 x 150 x 147 cm

Facing page:
Red Bamboo Reeds (detail), 2024
241 x 597 x 183 cm

Following spread:
Jet and Crimson Fiori (detail), 2024
178 x 168 x 135 cm

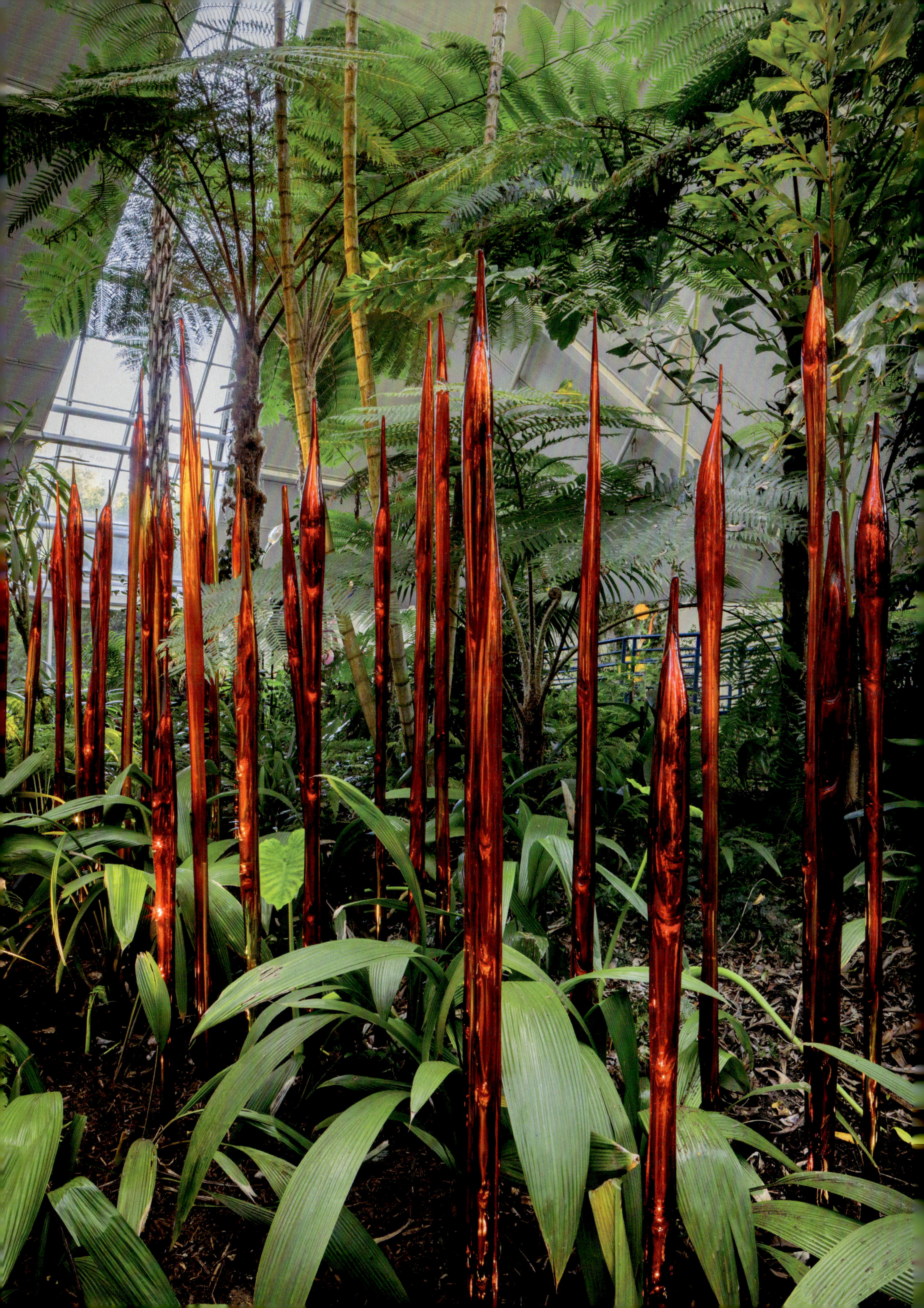

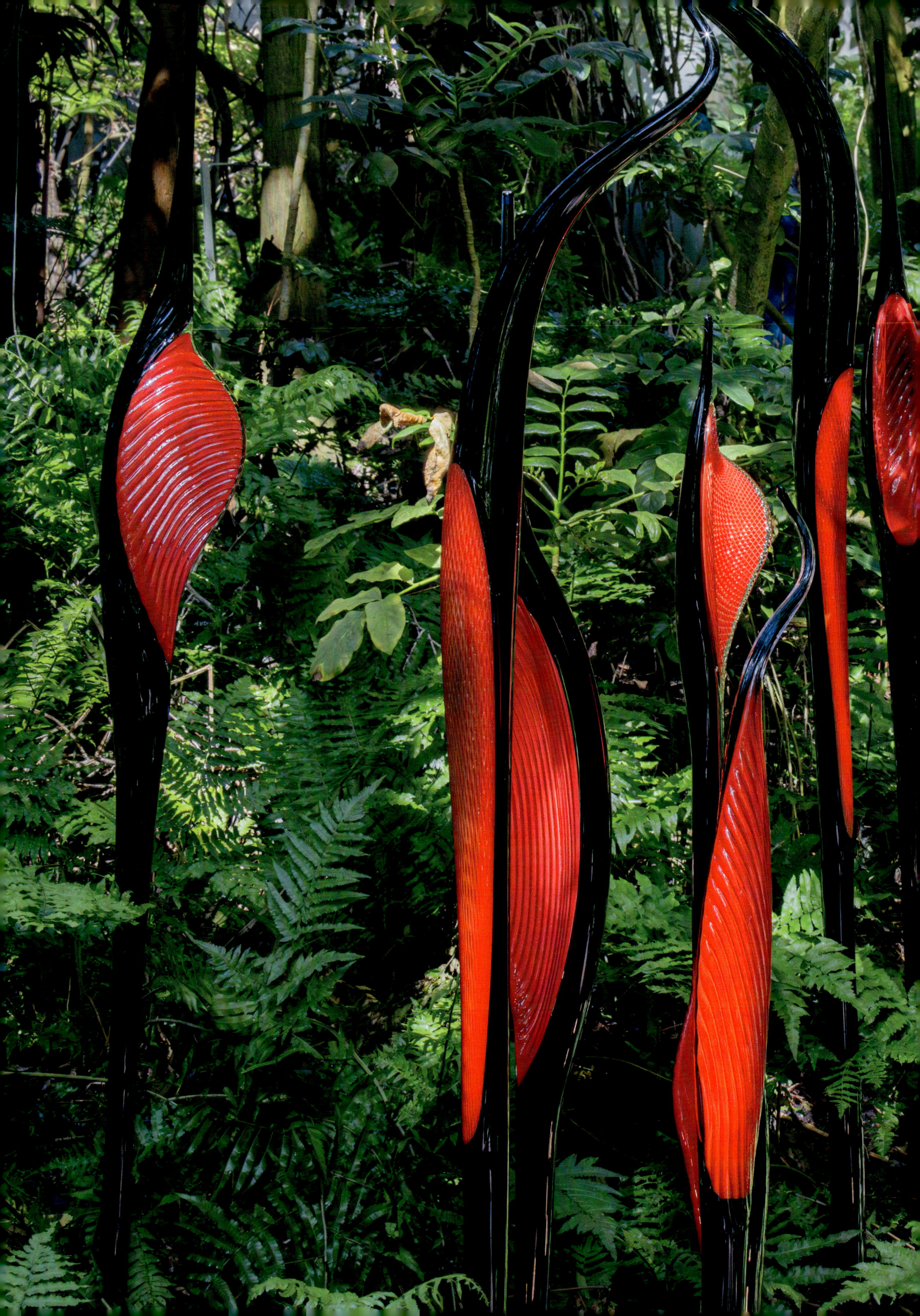

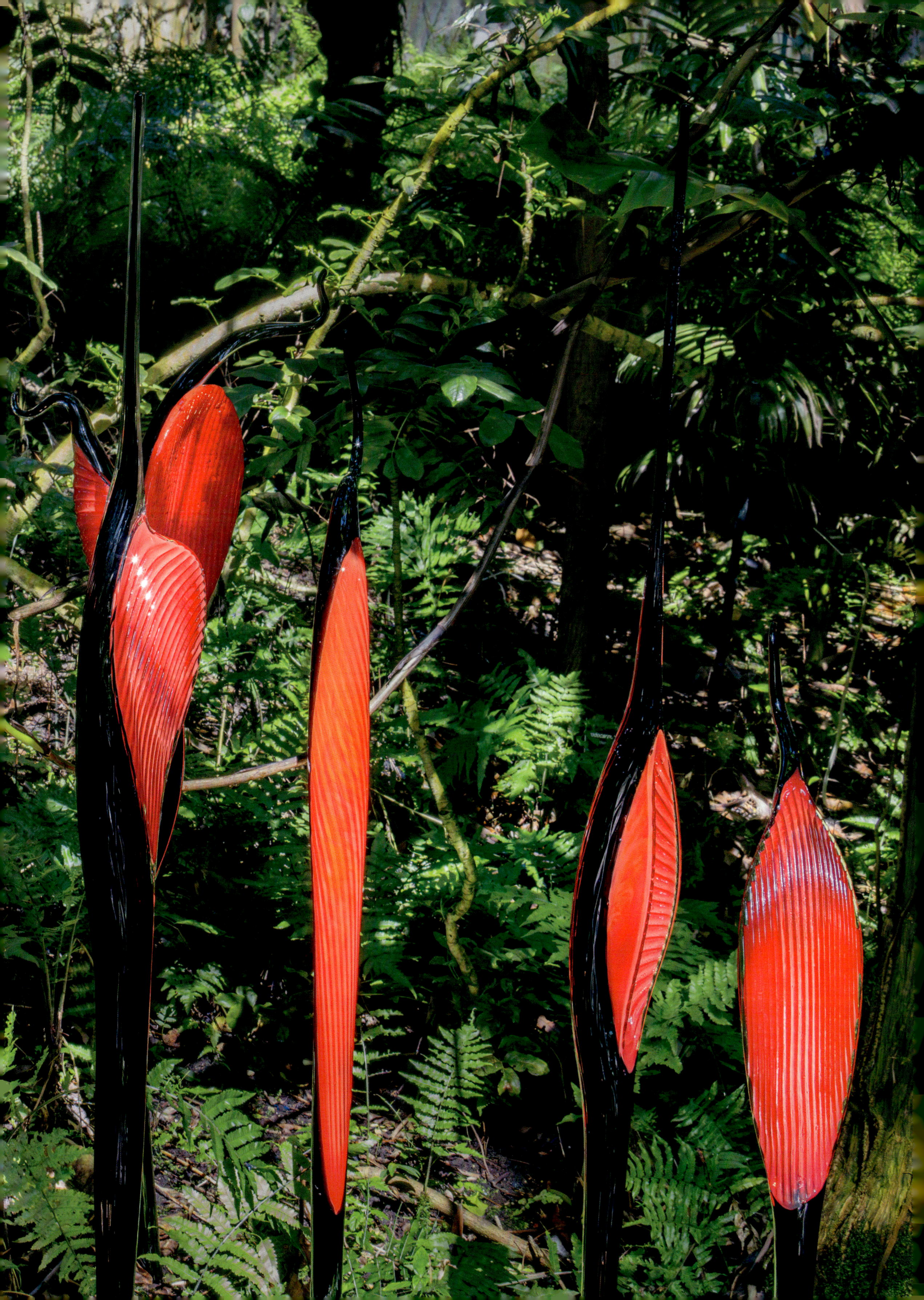

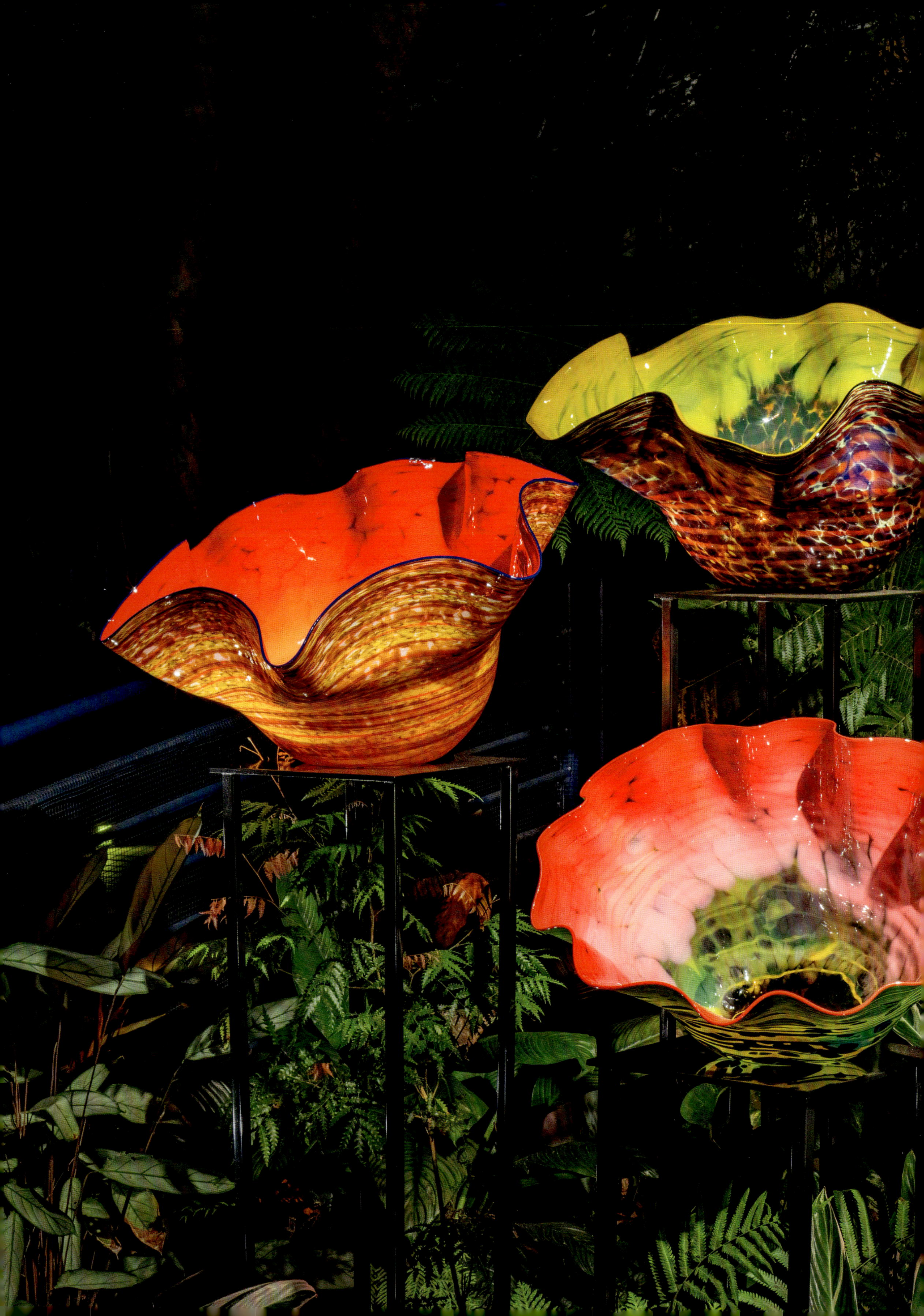

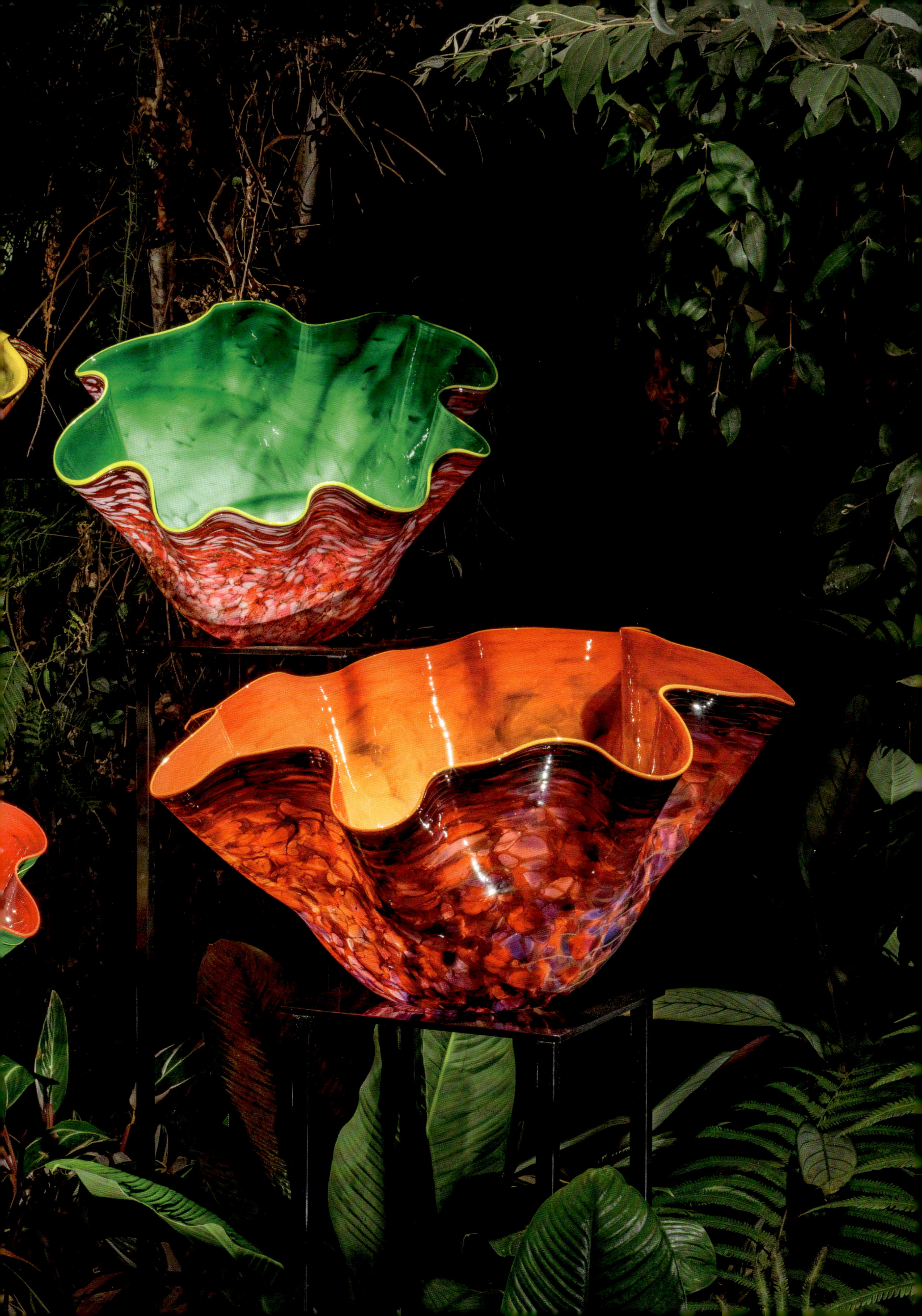

Previous spread:

Macchia Forest (detail), 2024

Facing page:

(left) *Tango Rose Ikebana with Pink and Indigo Stems*, 2001
152 x 86 x 46 cm

(right) *Mottled Onyx Ikebana with Clear and Gilt Stems*, 2009
152 x 56 x 38 cm

Following spread:

Red Bulbous Reeds (detail), 2022
193 x 399 x 302 cm

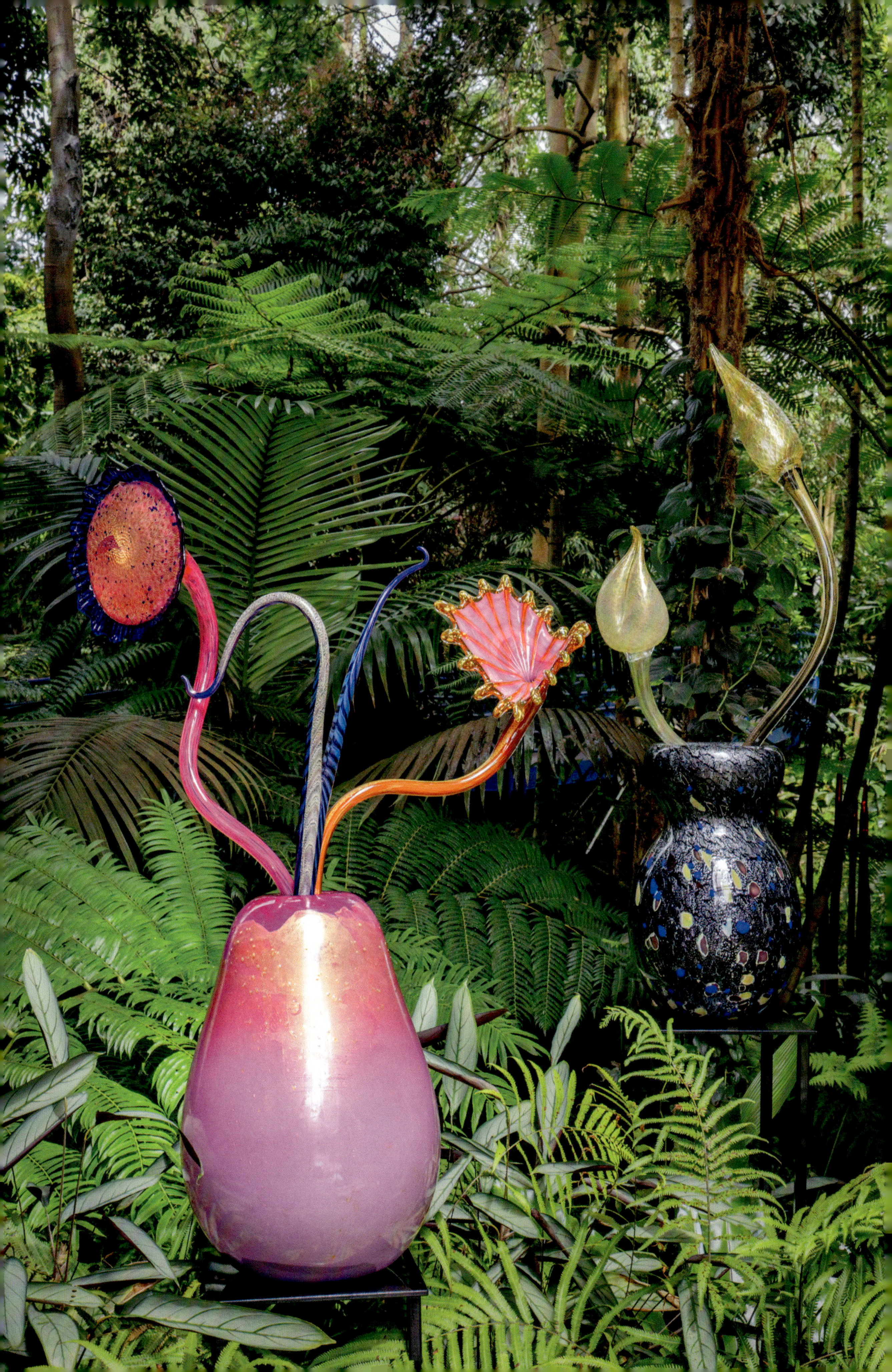

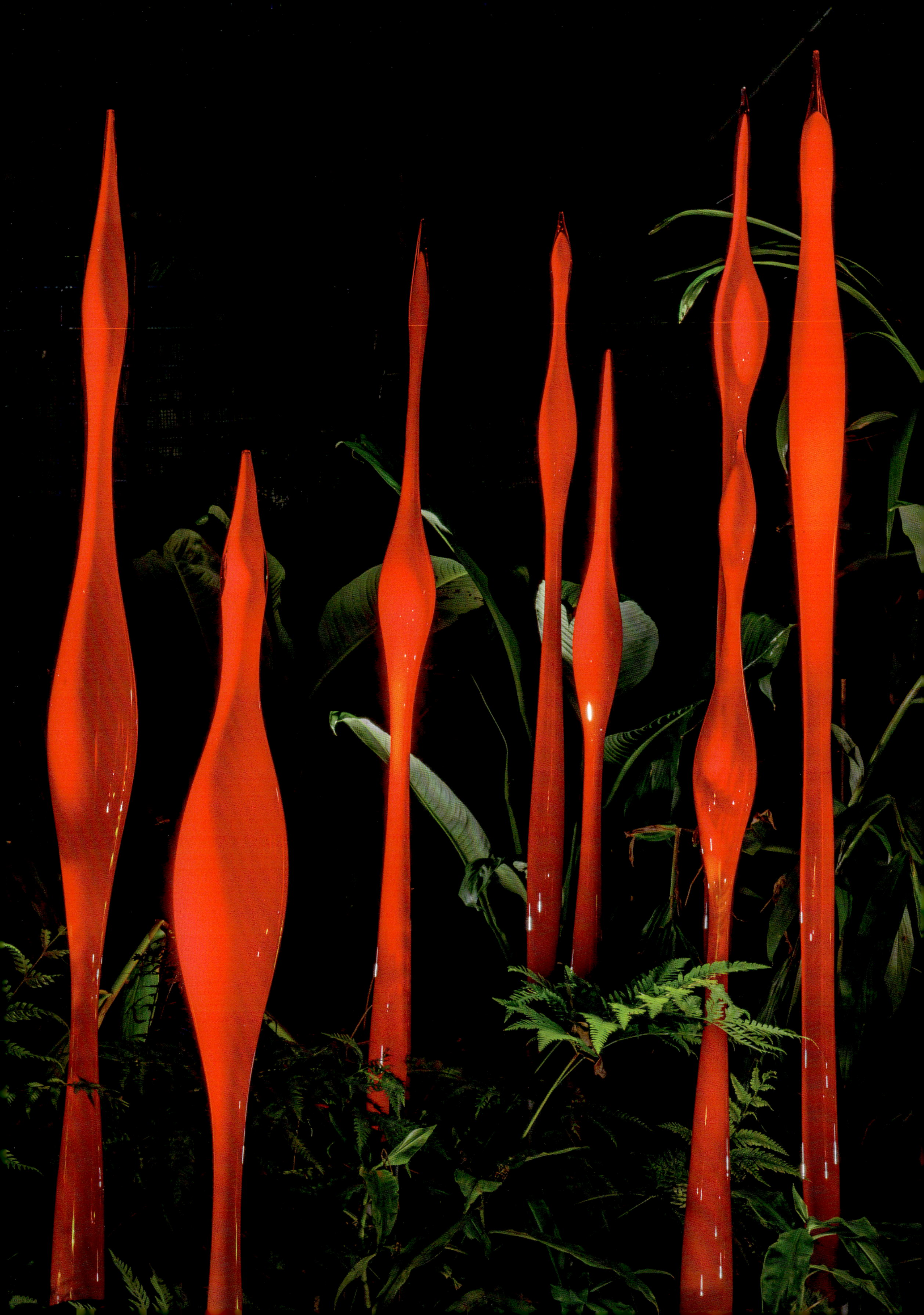

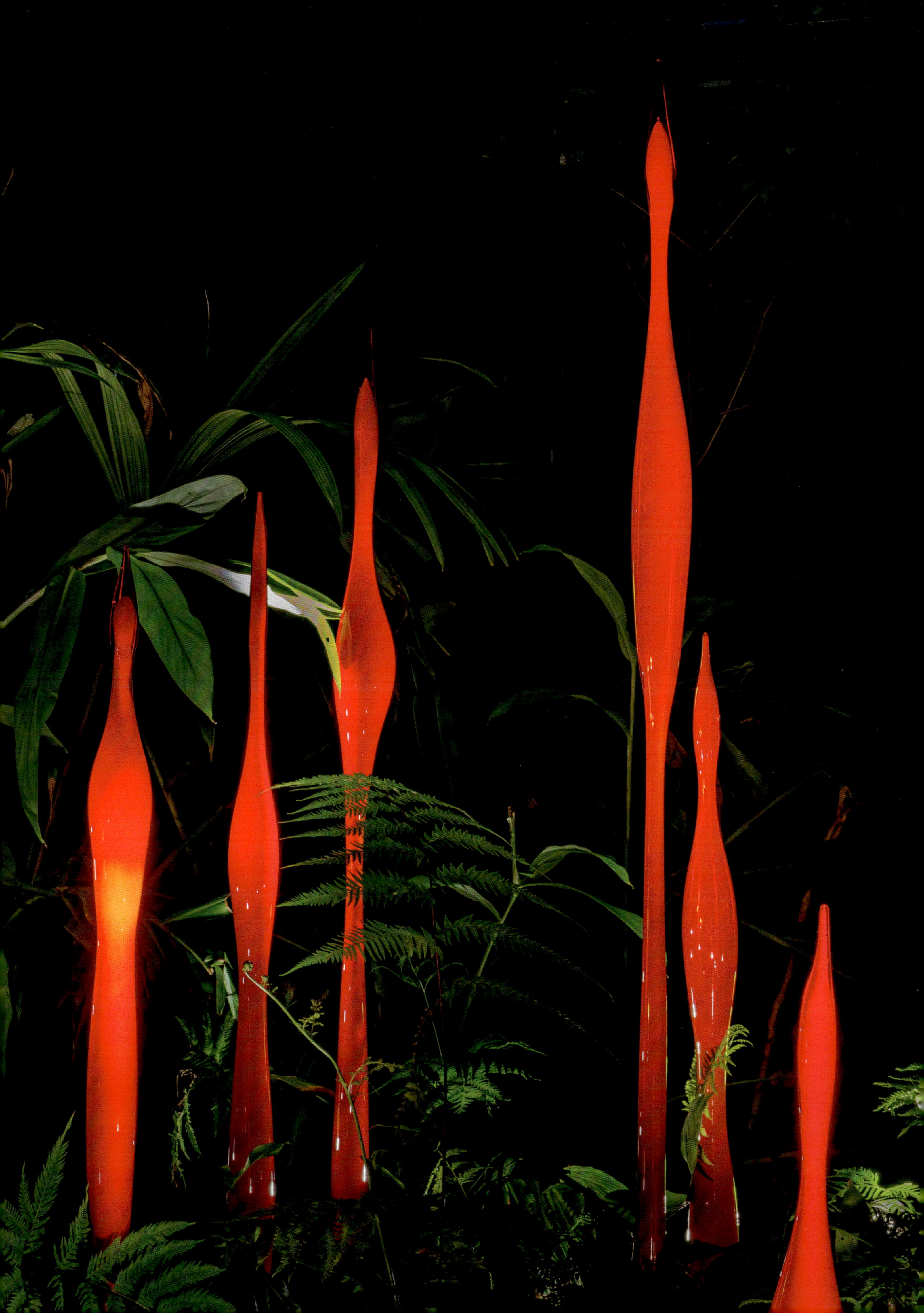

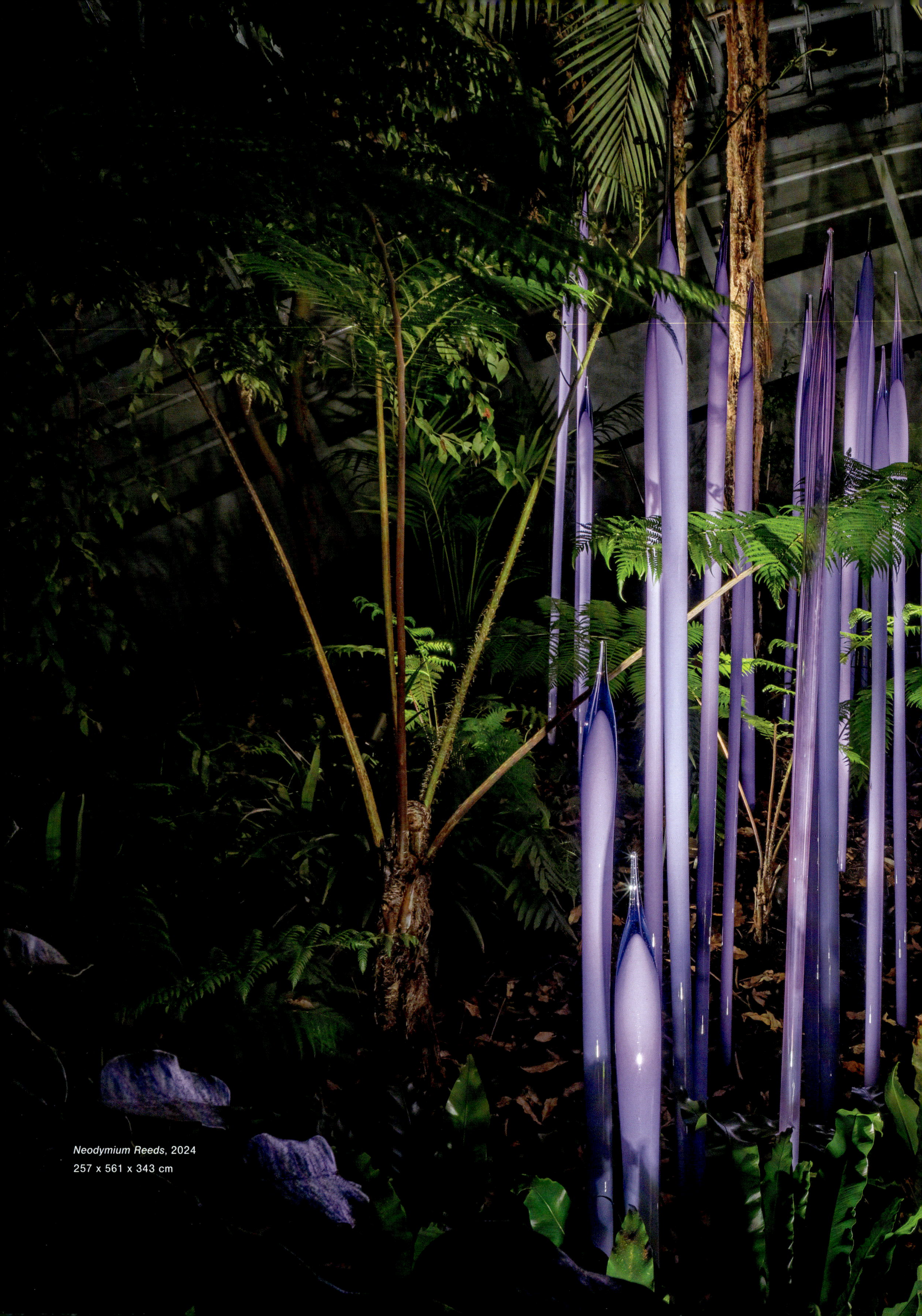

Neodymium Reeds, 2024
257 x 561 x 343 cm

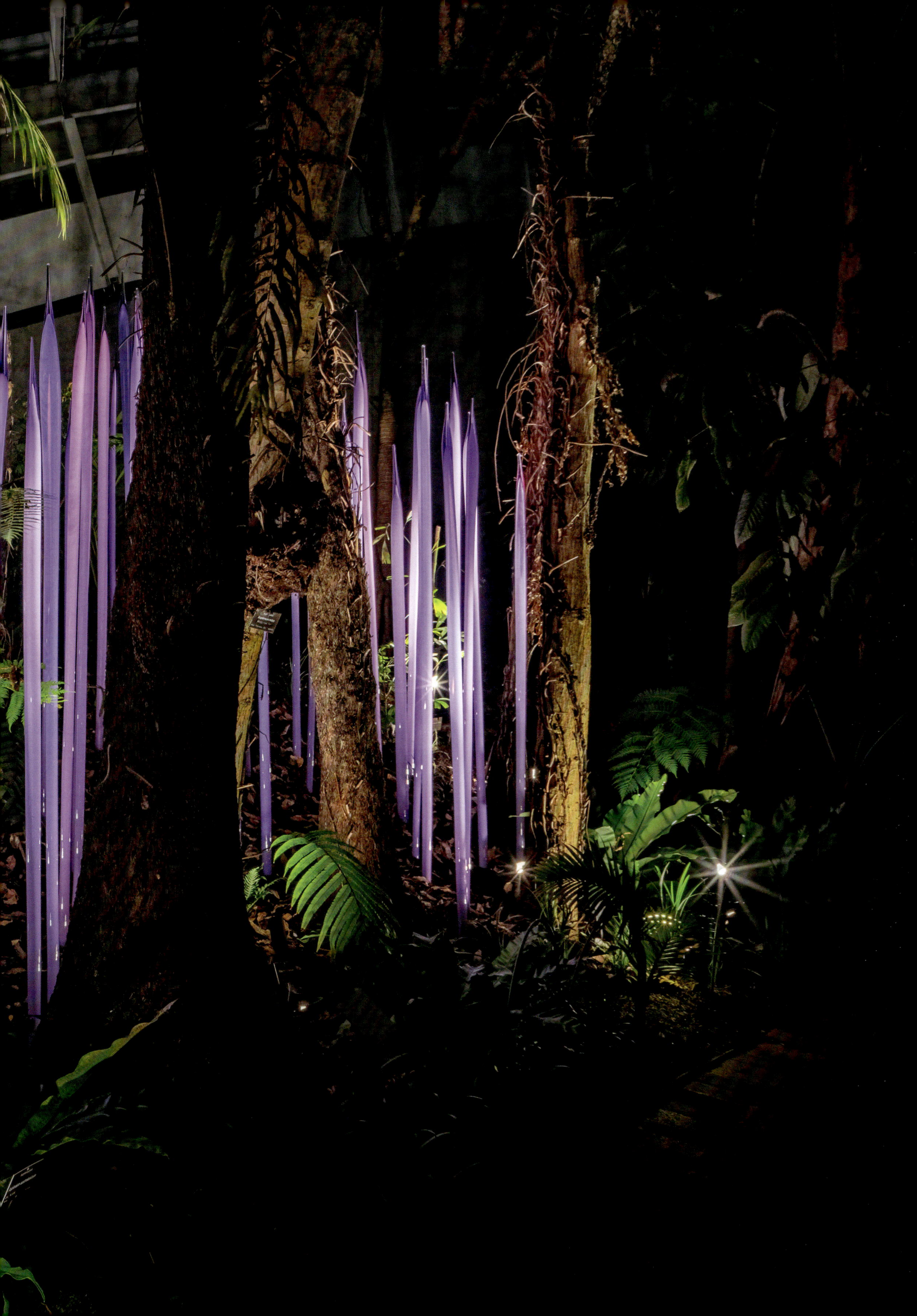

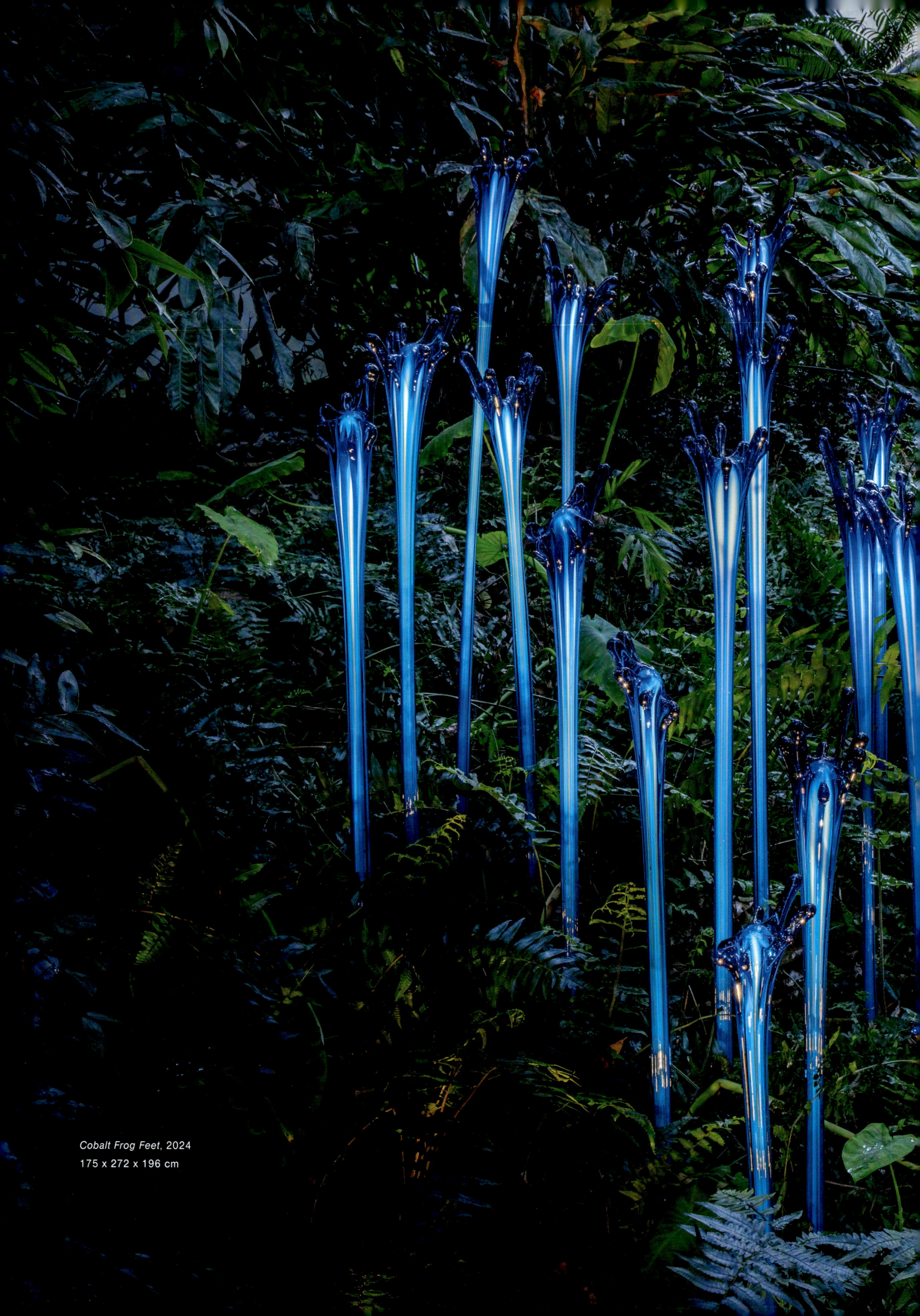

Cobalt Frog Feet, 2024
175 x 272 x 196 cm

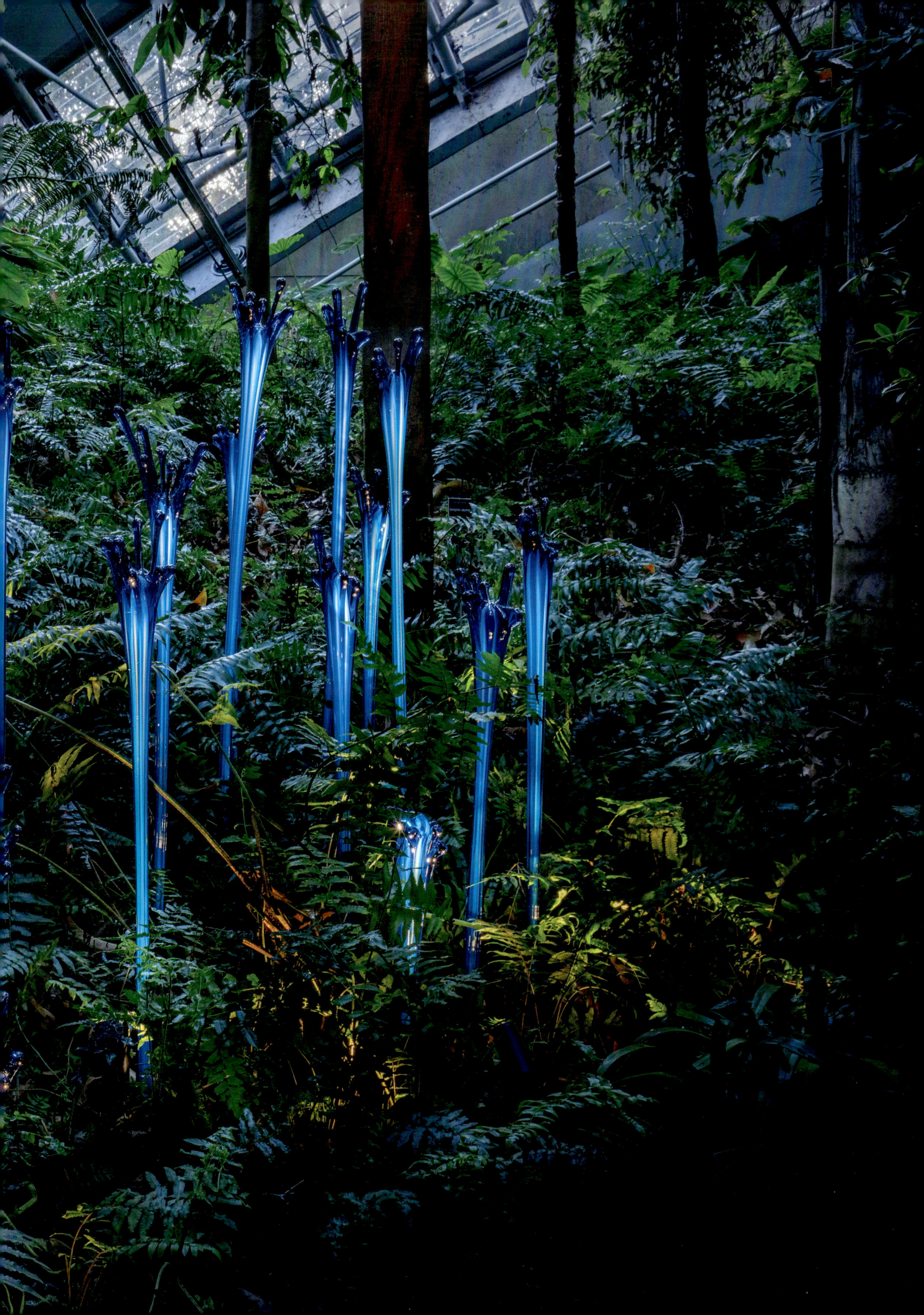

Glass in the landscape: The infinite affinities of form

Tim Richardson

Vivid Lime Icicle Tower, 2022
622 x 244 x 244 cm

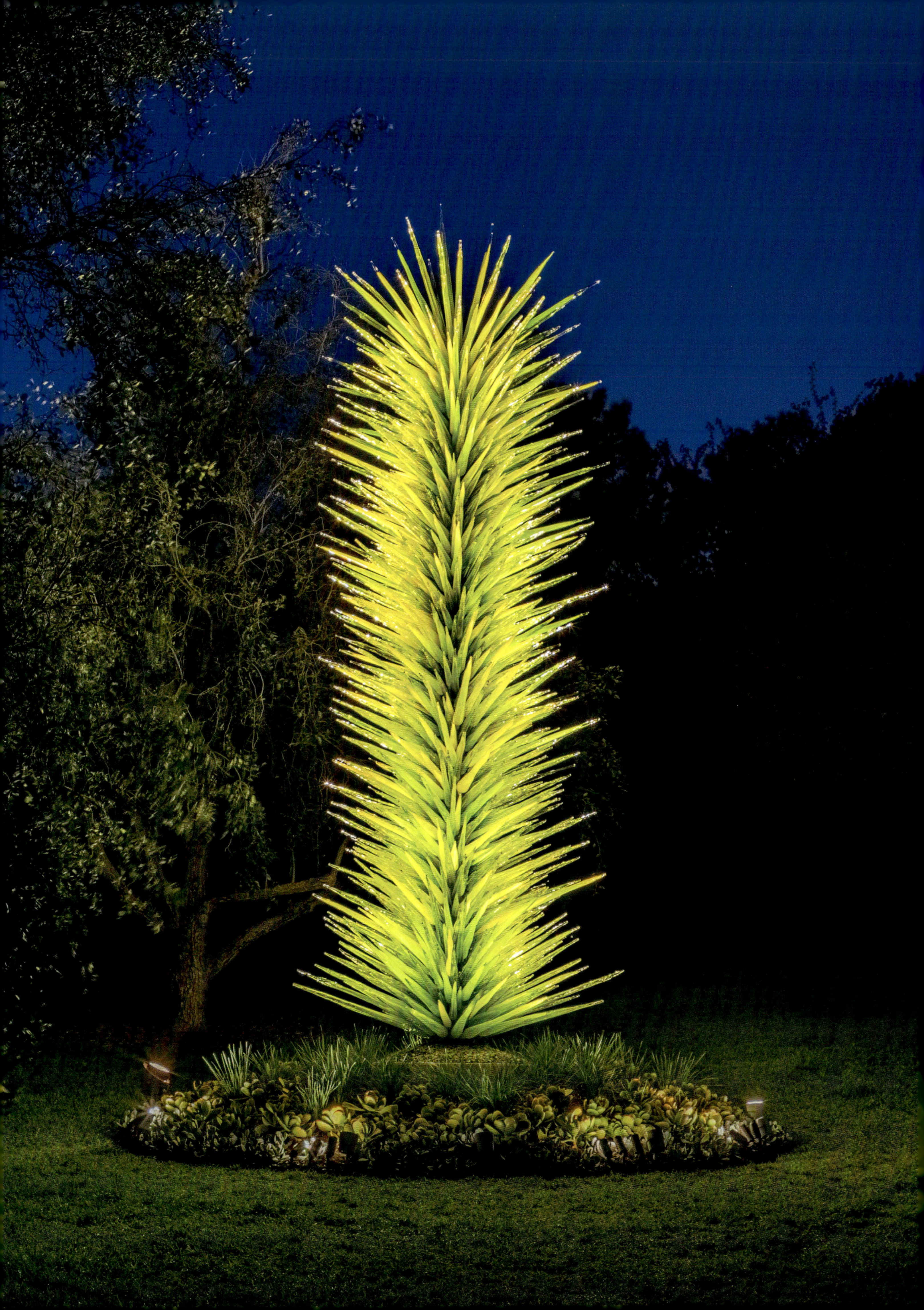

The genesis of Dale Chihuly's ongoing *Garden Cycle* (2001 to date) lies in the artist's interest in and appreciation of historical glasshouses. On one level, it was simply the thrill of exhibiting 'glass inside glass' that first drew him to formal botanic garden environments. But that interest soon developed into something much deeper and more enduring: a series of exhibitions set in a range of different garden environments, each of which takes the form of episodic installations of glass sculpture, all of which are distinctive and unique to a specific place.

The obvious affinities between Chihuly's glass works and the manifold natural forms of plant life remain perhaps the most striking feature of the series as a whole. But in addressing these exhibitions on the scale of landscape—which is how they came to be conceived—it becomes clear that Chihuly and his team expend just as much time, care and thought on the rhythm of the experience, on the atmospheric or tonal particularities of each setting within the whole landscape, as they do on the smaller-scale juxtaposition of art objects and plants.

For these exhibitions to be successful, visitors ought to be able to leave with a strong and satisfying sense that they have been immersed in a variety of glass/garden episodes that have somehow coalesced into an overall picture. The success of this is most dependent not on detail but on the manner in which the glass installations or episodes are set within the garden. The *Garden Cycle* has been successful partly because Chihuly responds to the individual particularities of each place and sites his own works in sympathy with it, so that they complement the landscape and collaborate with it, rather than simply utilising it as a backdrop (which has been the general tradition of siting sculpture in gardens since the early twentieth century).

While each exhibition in the *Garden Cycle* thus far has contained works specially fabricated in response to the site, the works on view in these exhibitions cannot in general be described as 'site-specific,' in that they include pieces from the same sets or series, either repeated or presented as variations on themes. On the other hand, some of the power of the *Garden Cycle* as a whole derives from the idea that a new artistic taxonomy—in this case, an artistic classification based on Chihuly's various glass series—has been imposed on the scientific taxonomy of the natural world that is historically associated with botanic gardens. So while site-specific is certainly the contemporary fashion when it comes to commissioning works for landscape settings, in the case of Chihuly's work there is no obvious advantage in its being conceived in this way. His work in glass complements the surrounding plant life, but not by means of 'blending in' with it. In that sense, it has been quite appropriate to develop a range of different series of glass forms for use in disparate situations—just as plants crop up in different environments in the wild.

Equally, Chihuly's art is possessed of such material consistency and elemental power that it can stand up to a landscape setting in its own right, existing genuinely in balance with it. The sense of the autonomy of Chihuly's works is exaggerated by the bold notion of spreading them all the way across the botanic gardens involved in the *Garden Cycle*—which was quite a leap of faith for many of the institutions, because it meant decisively altering the character of the garden for a number of months. An awareness of the temporary nature of the exhibitions was an important aspect of their transformative—and arguably transcendent—power, since each provides those familiar with that garden with a once-in-a-lifetime experience. All the curators of the scientific institutions involved thus far should be congratulated for their role in fostering such an ambitious crossover experiment.

Indoor art exhibitions have long been regarded as appropriate distractions in botanic gardens, generally taking the form of works on paper—most often, botanical illustrations. Outdoor art exhibitions and permanent installations are a more recent phenomenon in botanic gardens, a reflection of the growing popularity of dedicated sculpture gardens in the later twentieth century.

The exhibitions in Chihuly's *Garden Cycle*, however, stand apart from other ventures in that they represent an artistic marriage between the work of a single artist and the entire fabric of a single garden. Chihuly's works are not simply scattered about; they are enmeshed and interwoven with the place itself—with the topography, the buildings, the ponds, the roads and pathways, and of course the plants. As a result, the artworks not only respond to their settings but are palpably enriched by them. Emplaced as episodes within the wider landscape, they can play a role, too, within vistas, acting as new and exciting punctuation marks in the rhythm of the garden, while also colonizing perhaps unlikely features such as lakes,

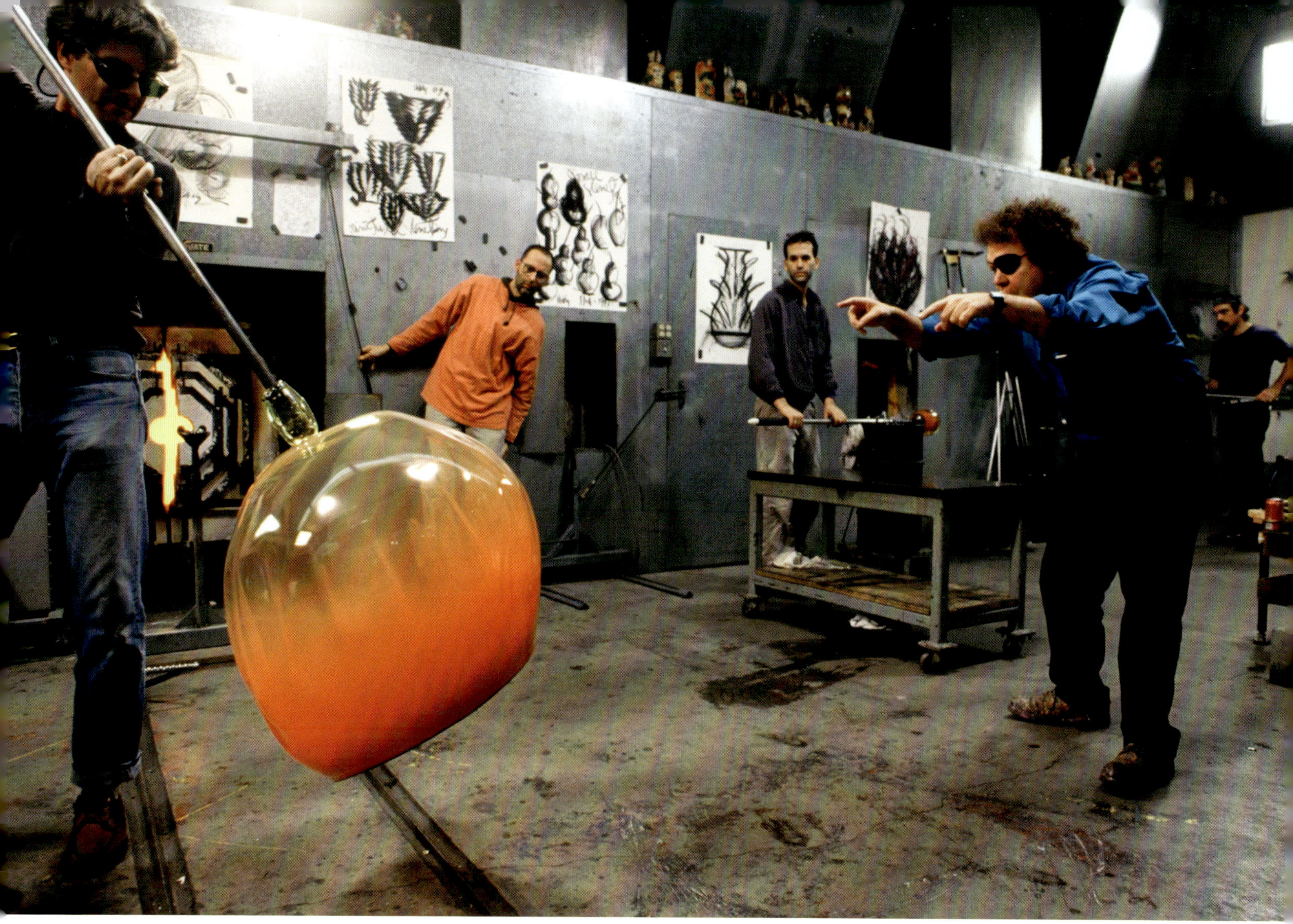

rockeries and formal Japanese gardens. It is this comprehensive, immersive quality that sets the *Garden Cycle* apart from a 'regular' sculpture-in-the-garden event.

The exhibitions in the *Garden Cycle* also enact a performative role, reinstating a tradition of wonderment in garden design that is evocative of the fêtes champêtres of Louis XIV's Versailles, where sculptural, automotive, musical or light shows dazzled and impressed visitors in the wooded bosquets on either side of the Grand Canal. As with Chihuly's garden exhibitions, there were set routes to follow around the gardens at Versailles. The nocturnal openings that are a feature of most of Chihuly's *Garden Cycle* exhibitions enhance this sense of drama and occasion, as regular visitors are enchanted to find a familiar and much-loved garden transformed by glowing artworks in colored glass. Seeing the glass lit at night is a completely different experience from that of seeing it by day. In the festive atmosphere of night, it is as if the gardens are there to be admired in their party dress, like a debutante who at long last has the chance to go to the ball.

For example, at the Royal Botanic Gardens, Kew, in southwest London in 2005–6, the focus of the exhibition was the celebrated Temperate House, designed by Decimus Burton in 1859 and an icon of glasshouse design worldwide. But that was just the beginning—there were also works that floated on the lakes or were placed at the ends of vistas and in various other glasshouses and buildings. There was, in fact, Chihuly glass sculpture everywhere. If there were any concerns that regular visitors might regard this 'invasion' as some kind of desecration of the botanic garden—the repository, after all, of the botanical riches of the British Empire throughout the nineteenth century, and still the most important botanical institution in the world—these were soon dispelled by an overwhelmingly positive response from those who came.

The success of the Kew exhibition (which was extended due to public demand, like a number of others in the *Garden Cycle*), and the evident affinity of his work with plants, led Chihuly to drop everything else and embark on a concerted and still-continuing program of botanic-garden exhibitions, most of them in the United States. Chihuly deliberately sought out different kinds of gardens in various climate zones, to add variety and richness to the series. Working out of his warehouse-sized studios in Seattle, Chihuly and his glassblowing team have further developed a vocabulary of glass forms that can be deployed to good effect in garden settings: tall *Towers*, elegantly stooping *Herons*, thin *Reeds*, clamshell-like

Richard Royal, Charles Parriott, David Levy, Chihuly, and Brian Brenno, The Hotshop, The Boathouse, Seattle, 1993. Photo: Russell Johnson

Macchia, glittering *Chandeliers*, bulbs and boats floating on lakes and climactic *Suns*–gorgon-like balls of yellow and orange. Chihuly's glass is certainly not for the colour-phobic, which is perhaps why the work has been so warmly received by the garden audience–gardeners being, by and large, chromatic hedonists and unreformed sensualists.

These coloured, squirming, and writhing concoctions seem to reflect the fecundity and variety of plants in the wild, both in the violence of their coloring and in the unpredictability of their forms. It means that Chihuly's work–though clearly man-made–sits well alongside the expected delights of the tropical or temperate house. 'I love to juxtapose the man-made and the natural to make people wonder and ask, "Are they man-made or did they come from nature?"' he explains. There is something about the endless variation and mutation in Chihuly's work that gives it a tangible affinity with natural selection, particularly the plant world.

Chihuly's series of shapes have all been developed obsessively over decades, and multicolored 'mistakes' or mutations are displayed alongside more perfect examples, just as in nature. "I think a lot of it comes from the fact that we don't like to use a lot of tools," Chihuly says, 'but natural elements to make the glass–fire, gravity, centrifugal force. As a result, it begins to look like it was made by nature.' Few of the pieces are based on specific botanical forms, but there is no shortage of bulbous gourds, curly tendrils, and arching stalks.

Despite their obvious artificiality, the glass pieces seem to complement the plants extremely well. Chihuly has been developing–or evolving–these series since the 1970s, continually varying them and experimenting, and seeing them in a botanical setting does bring to mind the habits of plants in the wild: grouped in clusters or spread as if self-seeded, with small mutations and differences in size and shape. There are other similarities: glass objects, like flowers, are usually much tougher than they look; Chihuly's many studio failures 'die' just like plants in the wild; and different types of light can transform them. The frozen liquidity of glass as a material also seems appropriate in the moist, throbbing, fecund setting of the hothouse.

The work, in fact, emerges as analogous to that produced by the self-sustaining regimes of nature. The idea of 'evolution' in an artist's practice is an overused analogy, but it is perhaps pertinent here because variation, repetition, death (in the sense of material failure), and selection are constant themes in Chihuly's work. The idea of a series being perfected or finished is anathema to him. As he has stated of his *Macchia* series, "Like much of my work, the series inspired itself."

One or two British art critics have described Chihuly's work as vulgar–though for the most part approvingly. His works are not just colourful, they glow with colour, which can seem a little bit much to some gallerygoers. Garden visitors, however, actively crave intense color, so Chihuly's work is perfect for this environment. Nature tends to extremes, after all. And is there not perhaps the slightest frisson of danger bound up with Chihuly's creations? Coming across them, alone, in a botanic-garden setting, one can feel ever so slightly vulnerable when faced with their physicality, virility and explosive aura. Shouldn't these things be behind bars? Perhaps that is overstating the case, but there is certainly something thrilling yet almost disturbing about some of these objects, deployed as they are in a setting–a botanic garden–that one reasonably expects to be polite, ordered, rational and probably gentrified. The subversion of prevailing atmosphere is one of the ideas at play in the *Garden Cycle*.

It will be intriguing to see how the series develops further, as the variety of garden settings used as venues grows ever wider.

Tim Richardson is an independent garden and landscape critic and historian, based in London. He is the author of a number of books, including Vista: The Culture and Politics of Gardens *(2005),* The Arcadian Friends: Inventing the English Landscape Garden *(2007),* Avant Gardeners *(2008), and* Futurescapes *(2011).*

This essay is adapted from one that first appeared in Chihuly Garden Installations *(Seattle: Portland Press, 2011), 77–82.*

Polyvitro Chandelier **(detail), 2006**

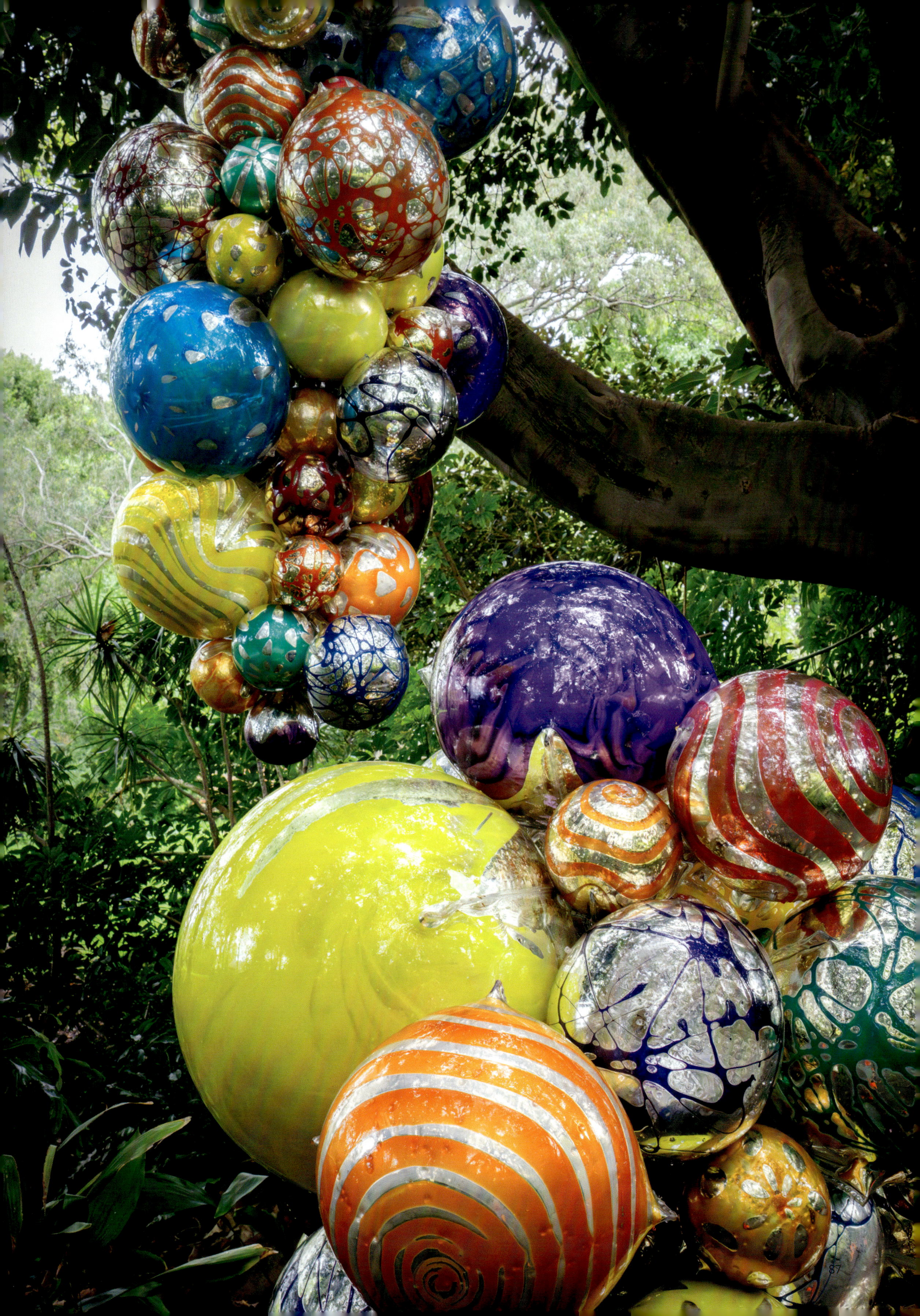

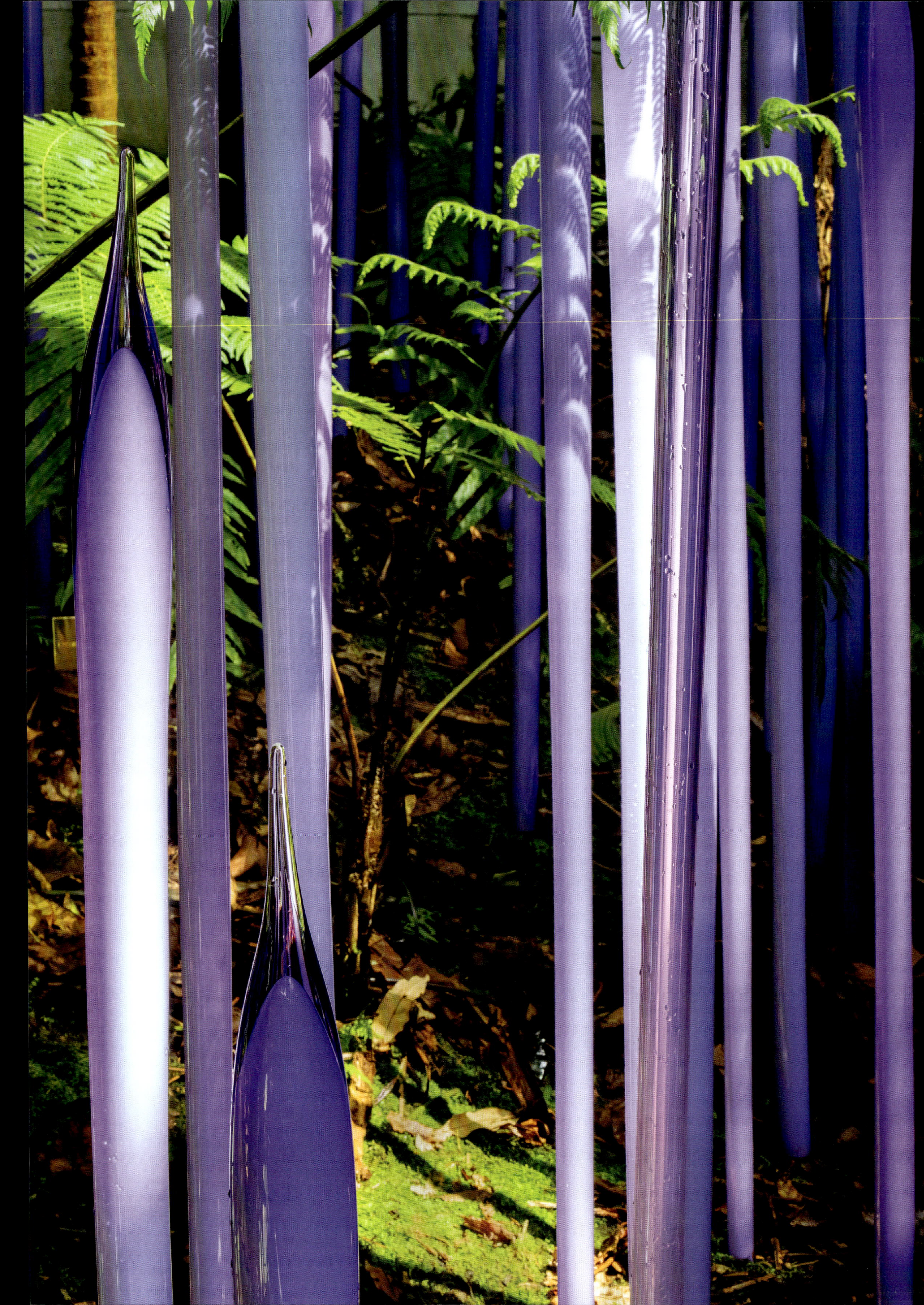

Born in 1941 in Tacoma, Washington, Dale Chihuly was introduced to glass while studying interior design at the University of Washington. After graduating in 1965, Chihuly enrolled in the first glass program in the country, at the University of Wisconsin. He continued his studies at the Rhode Island School of Design (RISD), where he later established the glass program and taught for more than a decade.

In 1968, after receiving a Fulbright Fellowship, he went to work at the Venini glass factory in Venice. There he observed the team approach to blowing glass, which is critical to the way he works today. In 1971, Chihuly cofounded Pilchuck Glass School in Washington State. With this international glass center, Chihuly has led the avant-garde in the development of glass as a fine art.

His work is included in more than 200 museum collections worldwide. He has been the recipient of many awards, including two fellowships from the National Endowment for the Arts and thirteen honorary doctorates.

Chihuly has created more than a dozen well-known series of works, among them *Cylinders* and *Baskets* in the 1970s; *Seaforms*, *Macchia*, *Persians* and *Venetians* in the 1980s; *Niijima Floats* and *Chandeliers* in the 1990s; and *Fiori*, *Glass on Glass* and *Rotolo* in the 2000s. He is also celebrated for large architectural installations. In 1986, he was honored with a solo exhibition, *Dale Chihuly: Objets de Verre*, at the Musée des Arts Décoratifs, Palais du Louvre, in Paris. In 1995, he began *Chihuly Over Venice*, for which he created sculptures at glass factories in Finland, Ireland and Mexico, then installed them over the canals and piazzas of Venice.

In 1999, Chihuly started an ambitious exhibition, *Chihuly in the Light of Jerusalem*; more than 1 million visitors attended the Tower of David Museum to view his installations. In 2001, the Victoria and Albert Museum in London curated the exhibition *Chihuly at the V&A*. His lifelong fascination for glasshouses has grown into a series of exhibitions within botanical settings. *Garden Cycle* began in 2001 at the Garfield Park Conservatory, Chicago, and continued at several locations, among them the Royal Botanic Gardens, Kew, in London, in 2005 and 2019; the New York Botanical Garden, Bronx, in 2006 and 2017; and Gardens by the Bay, Singapore, in 2021.

Chihuly has shown his work in solo exhibitions at museums including the de Young Museum, San Francisco, in 2008; Museum of Fine Arts, Boston, in 2011; Virginia Museum of Fine Arts, Richmond, in 2012; Montreal Museum of Fine Arts, in 2013; Royal Ontario Museum, Toronto, in 2016; Crystal Bridges Museum of American Art, Bentonville, Arkansas, in 2017; Groninger Museum, Groningen, the Netherlands, in 2018; and Artis—Naples, The Baker Museum, Naples, Florida, in 2020. *Chihuly Garden and Glass*, a major long-term exhibition, opened in Seattle in 2012.

Neodymium Reeds (detail), 2024
257 x 561 x 343 cm

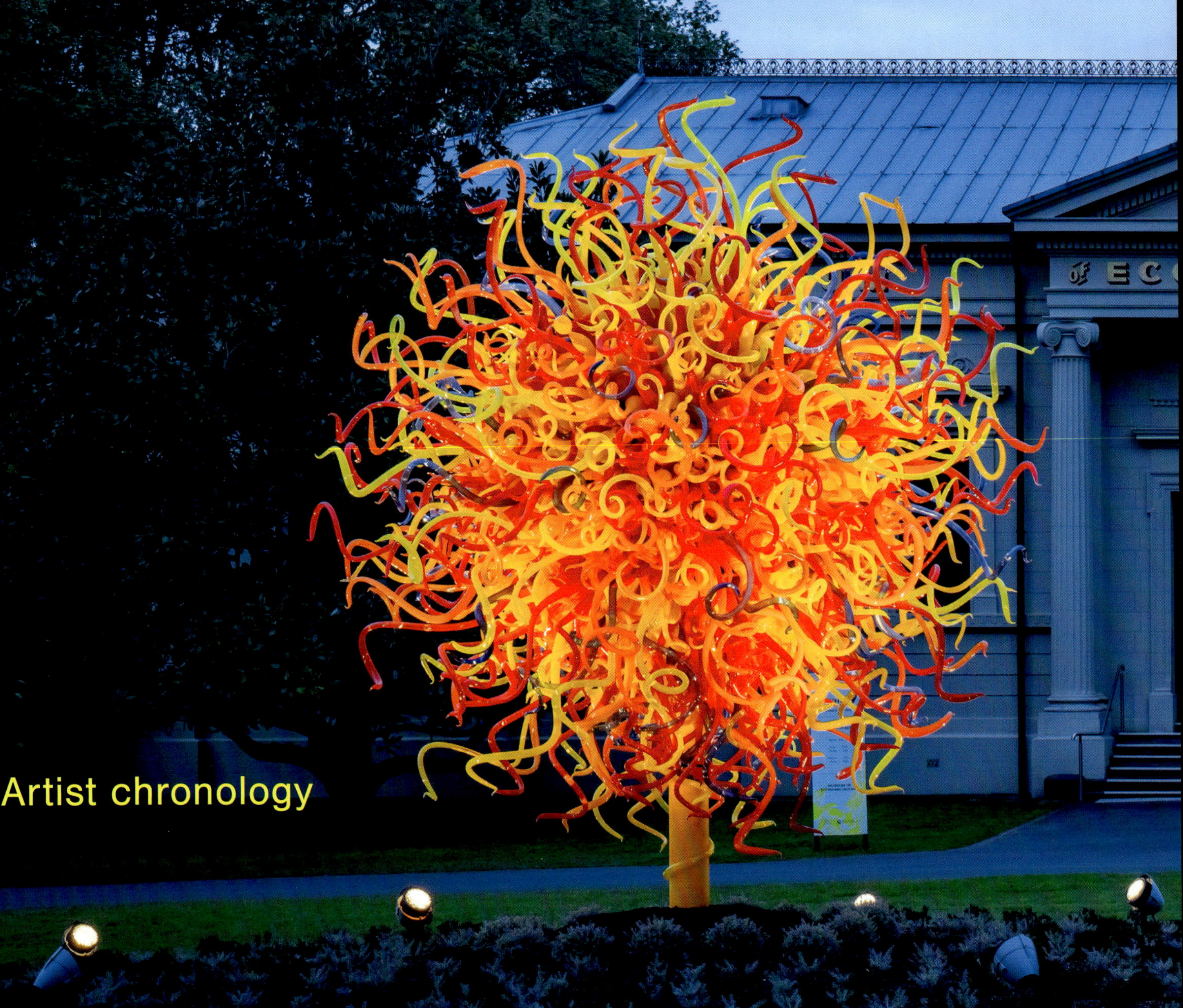

Artist chronology

1941 Born September 20 in Tacoma, Washington, to George Chihuly and Viola Magnuson Chihuly.

1957 Older brother and only sibling, George, dies in a navy flight-training accident in Pensacola, Florida.

1958 His father suffers a fatal heart attack at age fifty-one, and his mother has to go to work.

1959 Graduates from high school in Tacoma. Enrolls at College of Puget Sound (now University of Puget Sound) in his hometown.

1960 Transfers to University of Washington in Seattle, where he studies interior design and architecture.

1961 Joins Delta Kappa Epsilon fraternity and becomes rush chairman. Learns to melt and fuse glass.

1962 Interrupts his studies and travels to Florence to focus on art. Frustrated by his inability to speak Italian, he moves on to the Middle East.

1963 Works on a kibbutz in Negev desert, Israel. Reinspired, returns to University of Washington and studies interior design under Hope Foote and Warren Hill. In a weaving class with Doris Brockway, incorporates glass shards into woven tapestries.

1964 Returns to Europe, visiting Leningrad and making the first of many trips to Ireland.

1965 Receives BA in interior design from University of Washington. In his basement studio, blows his first glass bubble by melting stained glass and using a metal pipe.

1966 Earns money for graduate school as a commercial fisherman in Alaska. Enters University of Wisconsin at Madison on a full scholarship, to study glassblowing in the first glass program in the United States, taught by Harvey Littleton.

1967 After receiving MS in sculpture from University of Wisconsin, enrolls at Rhode Island School of Design (RISD) in Providence, where he begins exploration of environmental works using neon, argon and blown glass. Awarded a Louis Comfort Tiffany Foundation Grant for work in glass.

Artist Italo Scanga lectures at RISD, and the two start a lifelong friendship.

1968 Receives MFA from RISD. Spends the first of four consecutive summers teaching at Haystack Mountain School of Crafts in Deer Isle, Maine.

A Fulbright Fellowship awarded earlier in the year enables him to work and study in Europe.

Becomes the first American glassblower to work in the prestigious Venini factory, on the island of Murano.

1969 Makes pilgrimages to meet glass masters Erwin Eisch in Germany and Stanislav Libenský and his wife, Jaroslava Brychtová, in Czechoslovakia. Establishes the glass program at RISD, where he teaches for the next eleven years. Meets James Carpenter, a student in the Architecture Department, and they begin a five-year collaboration.

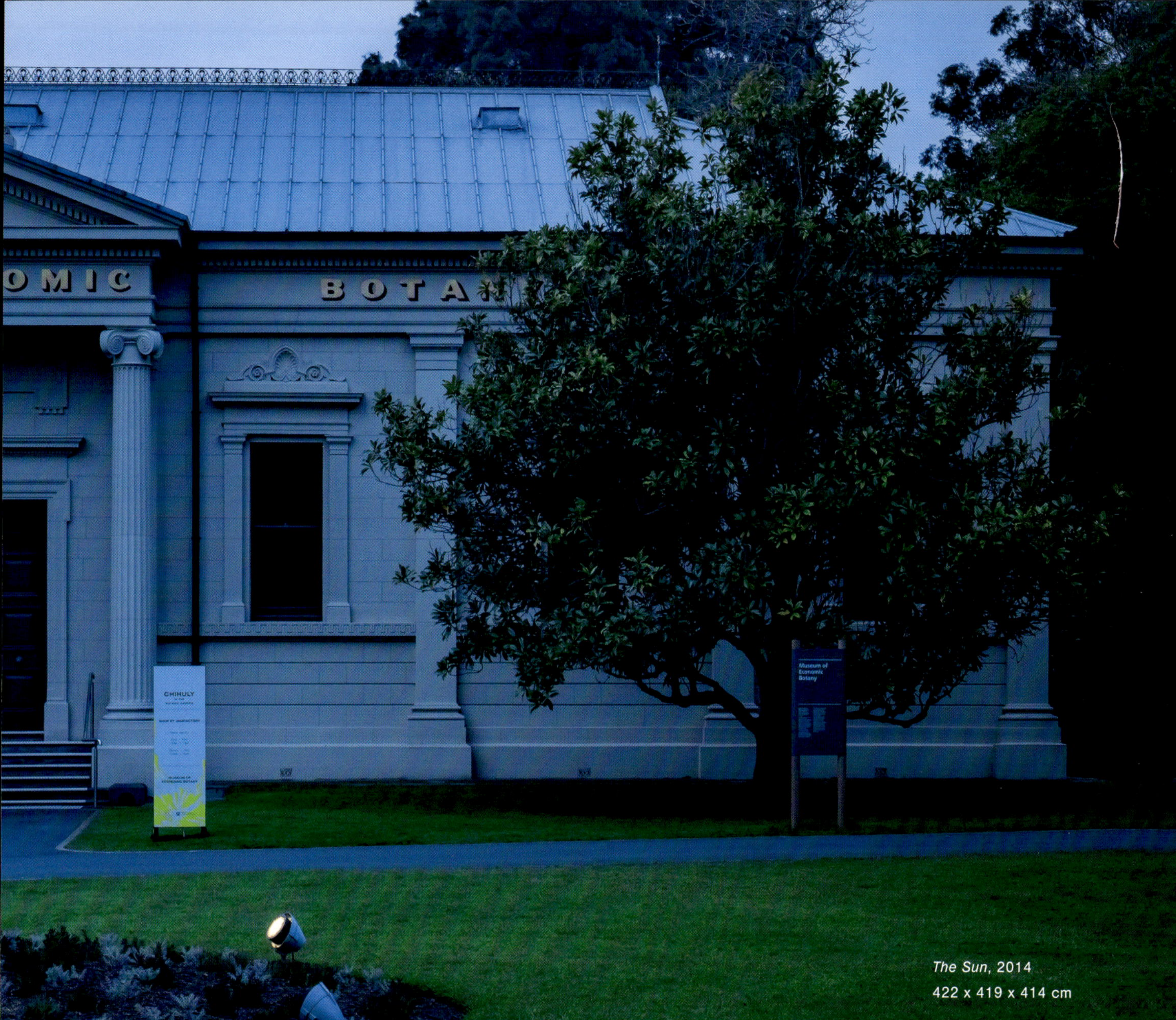

The Sun, 2014
422 x 419 x 414 cm

1970 While Chihuly and friends shut down RISD to protest the U.S. offensive in Cambodia, he and student John Landon develop ideas for an alternative school in the Pacific Northwest, inspired by Haystack Mountain School of Crafts.

1971 On the site of a tree farm north of Seattle owned by art patrons Anne Gould Hauberg and John Hauberg, the Pilchuck Glass School experiment is started. *Pilchuck Pond Installation*, Chihuly's first environmental work at the school, is created that summer.

In the fall, at RISD, he makes *20,000 Pounds of Ice and Neon*, *Glass Forest #1*, and *Glass Forest #2* with James Carpenter, installations that prefigure later environmental works by Chihuly.

1972 Collaborates with James Carpenter on more large-scale architectural projects over the next few years. They create *Rondel Door* and *Cast Glass Door* at Pilchuck. In Providence, they have a conceptual breakthrough with *Dry Ice, Bent Glass and Neon*.

1974 Works with James Carpenter and a group of students at Pilchuck to develop a technique for picking up glass thread drawings and incorporating them into larger glass pieces.

1975 At RISD, begins *Navajo Blanket Cylinder* series. Kate Elliott and, later, Flora C. Mace fabricate the complex thread drawings for his artwork.

He receives the first of two National Endowment for the Arts Visual Artists' Fellowships.

Becomes artist-in-residence with Seaver Leslie at Artpark, an annual arts program on the Niagara Gorge in New York State. Begins *Irish Cylinders* and *Ulysses Cylinders* with Leslie and Mace.

1976 An automobile accident in England leaves him, after weeks in the hospital and 256 stitches in his face, without sight in his left eye and with permanent damage to his right ankle and foot. After recuperating, he returns to Providence to serve as head of the Department of Sculpture and the Program in Glass at RISD.

Henry Geldzahler, curator of contemporary art at the Metropolitan Museum of Art in New York, acquires three *Navajo Blanket Cylinders* for the museum's collection–a turning point in Chihuly's career and the start of the artist's friendship with both the curator and the museum director then, Thomas Hoving.

1977 His *Basket* series–inspired by Northwest Native American baskets he sees at Washington State History Museum in Tacoma–is first made at Pilchuck with Benjamin Moore as gaffer and exhibited at Seattle Art Museum.

Continues teaching at both RISD and Pilchuck.

1978 Meets William Morris at Pilchuck, and the two begin a close, eight-year working relationship.

Another career milestone is a solo exhibition at the Renwick Gallery, a branch of the Smithsonian American Art Museum, Washington, D.C.

1979 Dislocates his shoulder in a bodysurfing accident and relinquishes the gaffer position for good.

William Morris becomes his chief gaffer for several years. Chihuly begins to make drawings as away to communicate his designs.

1980 Resigns his teaching position at RISD but returns periodically in the 1980s as artist-in-residence.

Begins *Seaform* series. Creates his first architectural commission: windows for Shaare Emeth Synagogue in St. Louis.

1981 Begins *Macchia* series.

1982 First catalogue is published: *Chihuly Glass*, designed by RISD colleague and friend Malcolm Grear.

1983 Returns to Pacific Northwest after sixteen years on the East Coast.

1984 Begins work on *Soft Cylinder* series, with Flora C. Mace and Joey Kirkpatrick executing the glass drawings. Honored as RISD President's Fellow at the Whitney Museum in New York.

1985 Purchases the Buffalo Shoe Company Building just east of Lake Union in Seattle and begins restoring it for use as his studio.

1986 Begins *Persian* series with Martin Blank as gaffer, assisted by Robbie Miller.

Establishes his first hotshop in Van de Kamp Building near Lake Union in Seattle. *Dale Chihuly: Objets de Verre* opens at Musée des Arts Décoratifs, Palais du Louvre, in Paris.

1987 Donates permanent collection to Tacoma Art Museum in memory of his brother and father (adding works to the collection years later in memory of his mother).

Marries playwright Sylvia Peto.

1988 Inspired by Italian Art Deco glass, begins *Venetian* series with Italian glass master Lino Tagliapietra, working from Chihuly's drawings; Benjamin Moore also plays a very important role, including translator.

1989 With Lino Tagliapietra and fellow glass master Pino Signoretto, as well as a team of glassblowers, begins *Putti* series at Pilchuck.

With Tagliapietra, Chihuly creates *Ikebana* series, inspired by travels to Japan and exposure to ikebana masters.

Purchases Pocock Building located on Lake Union, realizing his dream of being on the water in Seattle.

1990 Renovates his recently purchased building and renames it The Boathouse; it serves as studio and hotshop.

Returns to Japan.

1991 Begins *Niijima Float* series with Richard Royal as gaffer, creating some of the largest pieces of glass ever blown by hand.

Chihuly and Sylvia Peto divorce.

1992 Begins *Chandelier* series with a hanging sculpture at Seattle Art Museum.

Designs sets for Seattle Opera's 1993 production of Debussy's *Pelléas et Mélisande.*

1993 With Lino Tagliapietra, begins *Piccolo Venetian* series.

Creates *100,000 Pounds of Ice and Neon*, a temporary installation in Tacoma Dome.

1994 Creates five installations for Tacoma's Union Station Federal Courthouse.

Supports Hilltop Artists, a glassblowing program in Tacoma for at-risk youths, created by friend Kathy Kaperick.

Within two years, the program partners with Tacoma Public School District.

1995 An international project, *Chihuly Over Venice*, begins with a glassblowing session in Nuutajärvi, Finland, and subsequent blow at Waterford Crystal factory, Ireland.

1996 After a blow in Monterrey, Mexico, *Chihuly Over Venice* culminates with the installation of fourteen *Chandeliers* around Venice and a glassblowing session with Pino Signoretto and Lino Tagliapietra on Murano.

Creates his first permanent outdoor installation, *Icicle Creek Chandelier*, for Sleeping Lady resort in Leavenworth, Washington.

1997 Expands series of experimental plastics he calls *Polyvitro*.

Travels to Japan to blow glass at Niijima Glass Art Center and creates several temporary outdoor *Float* installations.

Travels with his team to a glass factory in Vianne, France, and they work with local glassblowers to create new works, some using industrial molds.

1998 Participates in Sydney Arts Festival in Australia.

A son, Jackson Viola Chihuly, is born 12 February to Dale Chihuly and Leslie Jackson.

Creates architectural installations for Benaroya Hall, Seattle; Bellagio, Las Vegas; and Atlantis, Bahamas.

1999 Begins *Jerusalem Cylinder* series with gaffer James Mongrain. Chihuly starts an ambitious exhibition, *Chihuly in the Light of Jerusalem 2000*, at Tower of David Museum of the History of Jerusalem. Just outside the museum, builds a sixty-foot-long wall made of twenty-four massive blocks of ice shipped from Alaska.

2000 Creates *La Tour de Lumière* sculpture as part of Contemporary American Sculpture exhibition in Monte Carlo. More than one million visitors enter Tower of David Museum to see *Chihuly in the Light of Jerusalem 2000*, breaking the world attendance record for a temporary exhibition during 1999–2000. Holds inaugural exhibition at Naples Museum of Art in Naples, Florida.

2001 *Chihuly at the V&A* opens at Victoria and Albert Museum, London.

Artist Italo Scanga dies after more than three decades as friend and mentor.

Chihuly in the Park: A Garden of Glass, at Garfield Park Conservatory, Chicago, begins *Garden Cycle*, a series of exhibitions in conservatories and gardens.

2002 Presents large-scale installations at Winter Olympic Games in Salt Lake City.

Chihuly Bridge of Glass is dedicated in Tacoma; conceived by Chihuly and designed in collaboration with Arthur Andersson of Andersson•Wise Architects, it is a pedestrian overpass featuring three permanent installations of Chihuly's work.

2003 Begins *Fiori* series with gaffer Joey DeCamp and creates first *Mille Fiori*, for exhibition at Tacoma Art Museum. A garden exhibition opens at Franklin Park Conservatory, Columbus, Ohio.

2004 Orlando Museum of Art and Museum of Fine Arts, St. Petersburg, Florida, collaborate and present complementary exhibitions of his work. Installs garden exhibition at Atlanta Botanical Garden.

2005 Marries Leslie Jackson.

Installs garden exhibition at Royal Botanic Gardens, Kew, London.

Exhibits at Fairchild Tropical Botanic Garden, Coral Gables, Florida.

2006 Mother, Viola, dies at age ninety-eight in Tacoma.

Between April and June, begins *Black* series.

Presents exhibitions at Frederik Meijer Gardens & Sculpture Park in Grand Rapids, Michigan, and Cheekwood Botanical Garden and Museum of Art, Nashville.

Begins *White* series.

2011 Holds exhibitions at Museum of Fine Arts, Boston, and Tacoma Art Museum.

2012 Exhibits at Dallas Arboretum and Botanical Garden.

Chihuly Garden and Glass opens at Seattle Center; the long-term exhibition of the artist's work features gallery spaces, a sculpture garden, and a glasshouse designed by Chihuly.

Exhibits at Virginia Museum of Fine Arts, Richmond.

2013 Montreal Museum of Fine Arts holds exhibition of Chihuly art.

Begins *Rotolo* series with gaffer James Mongrain.

With Seaver Leslie, revisits the *Irish Cylinders* from nearly forty years ago with new *Ulysses Cylinders* inspired by the James Joyce novel.

2014 At Clinton Presidential Library and Museum, Little Rock, Arkansas, displays temporary installations.

Exhibition opens at Denver Botanic Gardens.

Shows the new *Ulysses Cylinders* at Dublin Castle in Ireland.

2015 An exhibition of Chihuly's drawings opens at Museum of Glass, Tacoma.

Toyama Glass Art Museum, in Toyama, Japan, commissions permanent installations of his work.

2016 Returns to Atlanta Botanical Garden. Exhibits at Royal Ontario Museum, Toronto.

His set for the opera *Bluebeard's Castle* appears in a production in Portland, Oregon.

2017 Creates a new series—*Glass on Glass*—by painting with vitreous-glass

the Naples Museum of Art), in Naples, Florida. *Laguna Murano Chandelier* is featured in the exhibition *Venice and American Studio Glass* at Le Stanze del Vetro, Venice.

Receives the L. David Pye Lifetime Achievement Award from the American Ceramic Society for his accomplishments in advancing the field of glass art.

2021 Presents exhibition at Gardens by the Bay, Singapore.

Pilchuck Glass School in Stanwood, Washington, which Chihuly cofounded, celebrates fiftieth anniversary.

Mounts exhibition at two desert locations: Desert Botanical Garden in Phoenix and Taliesin West in Scottsdale, Arizona.

2022 Returns with new exhibitions to the Community Library, Ketchum, Idaho, and Oklahoma City Museum of Art. *Chihuly: Roll the Dice*, a film about Chihuly's process, debuts at the Santa Barbara Film Festival

The Smithsonian Channel debuts *Master of Glass: The Art of Dale Chihuly*. Gardens by the Bay, Singapore, commissions *Ethereal White Persians* for its permanent collection.

2023 Returns to Missouri Botanical Garden, St. Louis.

Partners with the Princess Grace Foundation to celebrate innovation in sustainability through the Grace Influential Positive Impact Award and creates *Gilded Mediterranean Blue Venetian with Speckled Leaves*.

Installs *Lupine Blue Persian Wall* at Palmer Museum of Art, Pennsylvania State University, and *Vermillion Fiori Installation* at the Connector at Winthrop Center in Boston.

2024 Presents *Chihuly in the Botanic Garden* and *In Full Colour: Dale Chihuly* at the Adelaide Botanic Garden, South Australia

Acknowledgements

Projects like this do not come around often, and when they do, you can only hope that your collaborators are as creative and professional as Chihuly Studio. It was our pleasure working with the Seattle team at a distance–but even more so in having them at the Garden as part of our team. We thank Dale Chihuly and the Chihuly Studio team for the inspiration that drove this project and the vision and skills to make it a reality.

Sincerest thanks go to the community of partners and sponsors in South Australia that have come along on the journey with us, especially the SA Major Events Fund and the Department of the Premier and Cabinet, without which this project would never have been possible. Our colleagues at the Ministry for Tourism, JamFactory and the South Australian Tourism Commission have provided vital expertise and connections in glass art, art retail and interstate marketing. A special thanks must also go to the glass art community of South Australia, for supporting this project and continuing to inspire us with your practice.

This exhibition has benefited from the goodwill and generous support of project collaborators who lent their time and expertise in a myriad of ways. To those of you who provided hours of pro bono assistance, thank you.

Finally, we would like to acknowledge the work of the tireless staff and volunteers at the Botanic Gardens and State Herbarium (BGSH), many of whom have juggled multiple roles and responsibilities over this past six months. The BGSH is a multifaceted organisation and this project brought together multiple teams, each of which has brought its own unique skillset and expertise to the challenges of the project. The coming together of magnificent art and a beautifully presented garden is a shared achievement of which all teams can be proud.

PRINCIPAL PARTNER

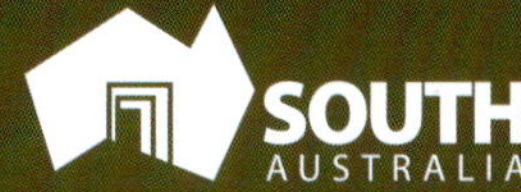

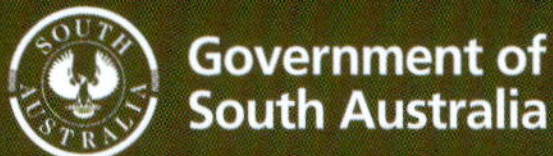

PRESENTING PARTNERS

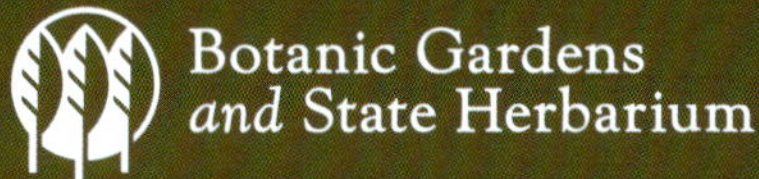

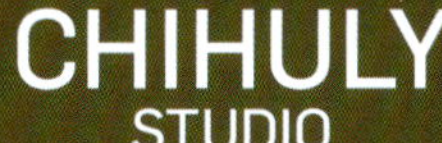

PROJECT PARTNER

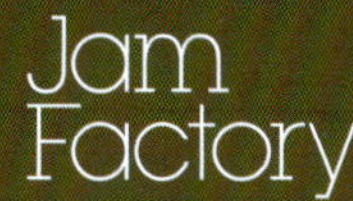

MAJOR PARTNERS

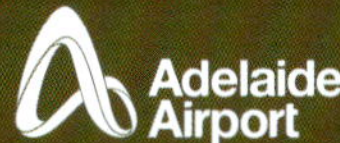

Minter Ellison.

FOODLAND
Great Food Lives Here

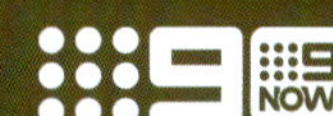

The Advertiser
Sunday Mail
We're for you

PARTNERS

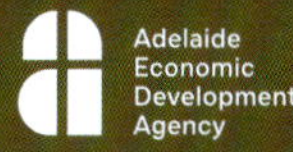

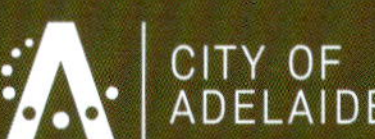

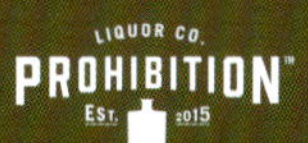

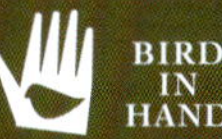

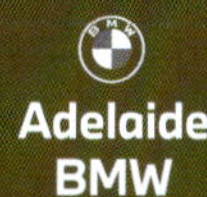

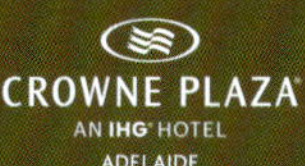

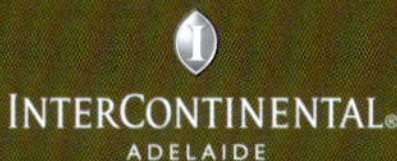

SUPPORTING PARTNERS

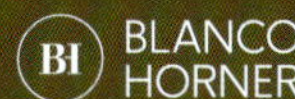

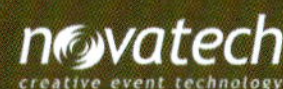

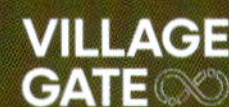

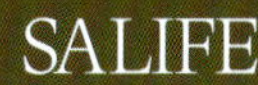

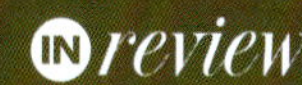

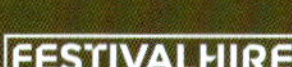

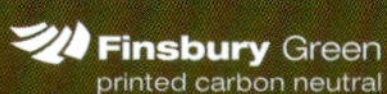

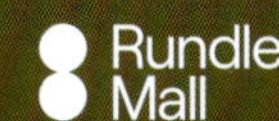

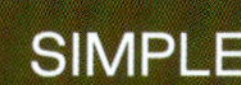

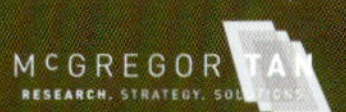

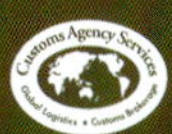

Division of
MONDIALE VGL

MEMBERSHIP PARTNERS

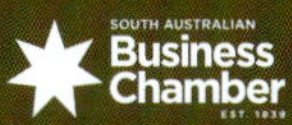

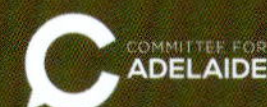

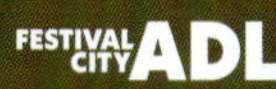

We would also like to extend our sincere gratitude to project collaborators Apollo Lighting for their tireless support and contribution to this project.

Published by Botanic Gardens and State Herbarium of South Australia

Goodman Building
Hackney Road,
Adelaide, South Australia 5000

www.botanicgardens.sa.gov.au

Published for *Chihuly in the Botanic Garden,* an exhibition organised by the Botanic Gardens and State Herbarium in cooperation with Dale Chihuly and Chihuly Studio.

27 September, 2024 – 29 April, 2025.

Authors: Hon. Peter Malinauskas MP, Michael Harvey, Brian Parkes, Leslie Jackson Chihuly, Tim Richardson and Lindl Lawton.

Design: Rachel Harris, Bit Scribbly Design

Producer: Rhianna Pezzaniti

Photography: Nathaniel Willson

Print: Finsbury Green, Thebarton, South Australia

ISBN: 978 1 922027 67 2

All works installed in the Adelaide Botanic Garden, South Australia, 2024
All dimensions are in centimetres in this order: height, width, depth

Cover images: Dale Chihuly, *Glacier Ice and Lapis Chandelier*, 2024.
338 x 170 x 170 cm